PURITY and PASSION

SPIRITUAL TRUTHS ABOUT INTIMACY
THAT WILL STRENGTHEN YOUR MARRIAGE

Purity *and* Passion

WENDY L. WATSON, Ph.D.

BOOKCRAFT

Library of Congress Cataloging-in-Publication Data

Watson, Wendy L., 1950-
    Purity and passion : spiritual truths about intimacy that will
strengthen your marriage / Wendy L. Watson.
        p.   cm.
    Includes bibliographical references and index.
    ISBN 1-57345-910-0 (alk. paper)
    1. Sex in marriage—Religious aspects—Church of Jesus Christ of
Latter-day Saints.   2. Church of Jesus Christ of Latter-Day Saints—Doctrines.
I. Title.
    BX8643.S49 W38   2001
    248.8'44'088283—dc21
                                                                    2001001647

Printed in the United States of America   72082-6785

10   9   8   7   6   5   4   3   2   1

For Brittney, Gabrielle, and Tyler

CONTENTS

ACKNOWLEDGMENTS

To thank all my family members and friends, colleagues and clients who have so generously influenced the writing, refinement, and publishing of this book would require yet another book!

How grateful I am to each of them for their wisdom, love, lives, and light.

I had loved before, but I knew not why.
But now I loved—with a pureness—
an intensity of elevated, exalted feeling,
which would lift my soul from the transitory things
of this groveling sphere and expand it as the ocean. . . .
I could now love with the spirit and
with the understanding also.

—Parley P. Pratt, *Autobiography of Parley P. Pratt,* 280

PURITY, PASSION, INTIMACY, AND TRUTH

After observing couples in all stages of their marital lives and providing thousands of hours of therapy to couples in distress, I've come to believe that personal purity is foundational to husbands' and wives' sexual satisfaction in marriage and fundamental to fulfilling their longing for love.

What else have I come to believe about intimacy?

• Purity and passion are perfect companions. They belong together.

• Purity increases and enhances passion.

• Passion that has been purified (which I call "pure passion") is always greater, in every way, than impure passion.

• "Pure passion" strengthens marriages and is key to true marital intimacy.

• Marital intimacy can be much more grand and more obtainable than many have believed.

• The Lord wants spouses to experience marvelous marital intimacy that creates life and love.

• The Lord blesses spouses who are willing to put aside the ways of the world in order to partake of true marital intimacy.

• The Holy Ghost enhances couples' marital intimacy because He will "increase, enlarge, expand, and purify all the natural passions and affections." (Parley P. Pratt, *Key to the Science of Theology,* 61.)

• When husbands and wives unite in "pure passion," in magnified marital intimacy, the enjoyment and love they experience is far beyond anything this world dreams of or represents as ideal marital intimacy.

What led me to these beliefs?

I've worked as a marriage and family therapist for more than twenty-five years. I've also spent two decades teaching, researching, and writing about marriage and family therapy, as well as supervising and consulting with other marriage and family therapists, nationally and internationally. Though I have never been married myself, I've had the privilege in the course of my life's work to learn from the best there are: real people with real challenges and real needs who really want to strengthen their relationships.

SOME COMMON PROBLEMS

The heartfelt concerns expressed to me by men and women who feel discouraged about, and in some cases even betrayed by, their marriages include everything from A to Z. Starting with "A," the effects of abuse, addictions, and adultery hold the intimacy in many marriages captive.

You may be among the fortunate who say, "Thank heavens those aren't our problems." But is there a challenge, a problem in your marriage that *does* concern you? Are there things about your relationship that make it less than what you hoped? What one thing would make the biggest difference in the strength of your relationship? And now, just for a moment, think about how your spouse would answer those same questions.

Perhaps you may even be saying, "We don't really have any problems in our relationship. I just think our marriage could benefit from a little more attention, maybe a little tune-up, so that we can enjoy even more intimacy."

Whatever the present state of your relationship, see if any of the following concerns about intimacy sound familiar. Because there are at least two sides to every problem, each spouse's perspective is provided:

1. "My wife doesn't understand how hard I'm trying to juggle everything. It's not great to come home to someone who lets me know I've disappointed her over and over again."

"My husband has time for everyone else, but he never has time for me."

2. "My wife controls my every move and everything about our home and family."

"My husband never takes any initiative when it comes to our marriage and family, and particularly to our children."

3. "I love my wife, but I don't think that just saying the words makes a difference. It doesn't to me. People say those words all the time and it means nothing. My wife should know I love her by how I treat her."

"I can't remember the last time my husband told me he loved me. It would really lift my spirits to hear those words from him. I've tried to get him to tell me but he just shrugs me off."

4. "My wife gives all her attention to our baby. Morning, noon, and night, she is riveted on what our daughter needs. I don't think she even knows when I'm home."

"My husband never understands that by the end of the day I'm tired of meeting everyone's needs and just want some time alone."

5. "My wife is so cold to me. I miss the days when she was so affectionate and loving."

"My husband never talks to me. I long for the days when we used to talk about everything and anything."

6. "My wife isn't willing to support me when I have to go to business conventions and social gatherings. She stands off to the side and almost snickers at the 'pomp and circumstance,' as she calls it. I wish she would be willing to enter into my world sometimes. I love having her there with me, but when she acts like that I just go and do my own thing."

"My husband is so hesitant to even acknowledge me when we're with other people. If we're at one of his 'pooh-bah' affairs, he's off 'pressing the flesh' and working the crowd, and I'm left all alone."

7. "My wife never responds to anything I do or say. I have to yell to even get her attention."

"My husband says such cruel things to me. I don't know how much longer I can take it. I feel my spirit shrink when he comes into the room."

8. "My wife doesn't appreciate how hard I work and how difficult it is to provide for our family. I feel like I'm running scared much of the time. I try to plan ahead for our future. She wants to buy things that don't matter. It feels like she undoes everything I'm trying to do to bring security to our lives."

"My husband controls all our money. I feel like a kid again asking for an allowance. It's definitely *his* money and he lets me know it. He acts like what I do at home and with the children doesn't matter—and that it certainly is not as important as his next business deal."

9. "My wife wants to control everything I do, from what I watch on TV to when I come to bed at night. I need to do something to have a little fun in my life. She sure doesn't want to have any these days."

"I want to trust my husband and his judgment on things, but when I catch him watching something pornographic on TV, it just makes all my fears come back. He says there's nothing wrong with what he's watching, but he's so different when he comes to bed after watching that stuff. It really turns me off."

10. "My wife puts so much energy into everyone else and everything else, but she never has time for our marriage. I feel

like I would need to be a struggling person somewhere out in a third world country to catch her attention these days."

"I do more and more with my children and in the community because nothing is happening with my husband in our marriage."

11. "My wife wants me to be a 'spiritual giant.' Unless I'm basically General Authority material, she doesn't want anything to do with me."

"I feel so 'unequally yoked' with my husband. We really don't have the same goals. I feel like I want to go one way and he's pulling another. I am the one who has to bring up family prayer and scripture study and home evening. The real problem is that I don't respect him. I wish it were different."

12. "I always feel like my wife is punishing me for something. I know I wasn't very involved with our family when our kids were little. Marriage was a huge adjustment for me. I didn't know how to be a husband or a father—I never saw that growing up because my dad was more devoted to his work than to my mom and us kids. I also know my temper caused us problems. But that was years ago. I've read books and taken communication courses with my business. I'm ready to have a genuine, loving relationship with my wife but it always seems like she'll let me get only so close. Doesn't she see all the changes in me?"

"I don't know why I hold back from my husband. He's a good man, and I love him. But I just don't seem able to really give my whole heart to him. I guess I don't really trust my feelings with him."

13. "I need to hide how much it hurts me when my wife rejects me sexually. I've almost turned off my feelings because I can't stand the pain. I just feel numb most of the time."

"My husband wants to make love at the most inconvenient times. Like early in the morning when I feel under pressure to get the kids up and dressed and off to school, he wants to be Don Juan."

14. "My wife doesn't understand that until I feel love from

her inside the bedroom, I don't really feel loved by her outside the bedroom."

"My husband doesn't understand that until I feel love from him because of activities we share outside the bedroom, I don't feel like showing love to him inside the bedroom."

15. "I feel even more lonely now than when I was single."

"Is this all there is to marriage?"

CHANGE IS POSSIBLE

As I have reflected on these and other intimacy struggles, I've come to believe that change is always possible. I've watched couples draw closer together, enliven relationships that are flat, and heal old wounds so they can enjoy what I refer to as true marital intimacy—some of them, for the very first time. It is because of these husbands and wives—my heroes and heroines—that I'm passionate about purity and passion, about true marital intimacy.

Because of the increased light and knowledge about life and love and intimacy that we've been given in The Church of Jesus Christ of Latter-day Saints, I believe we can and even should be the most loving people on earth. We can have marriages that are gloriously intimate in every way—spiritually, mentally, emotionally, and, of course, physically. Achieving that kind of closeness is a process. But it really is possible.

I believe that husbands and wives can seek to become increasingly pure by coming out of the world, leaving behind Lucifer's distortions of love, and laying down other impurities such as anger, unrighteous dominion, resentment, unforgiveness, pride, dishonesty, and blatant sin. I believe that as couples come closer to the Savior, they can experience more joy and power and peace and comfort and light and love and truth in their marriages. Indeed, I believe that as husbands and wives increase their personal purity, there will be enough and to spare of all they have been longing for within their marriages.

WHAT I HOPE

Because I believe that personal purity is the key to passion—the kind of passion that strengthens marriages and is vital for true marital intimacy—I believe that in some sense, regardless of our present marital status, we are all preparing for strong marriages and grand moments of marital intimacy. The more pure our thoughts and words, our feelings and actions, the more grand and expanded is the purified passion we will be able to offer, and the greater will be our enjoyment.

Joseph Smith taught the connection between increasing purity and increasing enjoyment in life: "The nearer a man approaches perfection, the clearer are his views, and the greater his enjoyments, till he has overcome the evils of his life and lost every desire for sin." (*Teachings of the Prophet Joseph Smith,* 51.)

Whether you have been married for forty years, have been remarried for four years, will be married in four weeks, or have never married, I hope that the ideas, experiences, invitations, and suggestions offered in this book will be useful as you prepare for and partake of marital intimacy.

My hope is that your views about intimacy will be lifted upward and become clearer as you read this book and reflect on the ideas offered. Some of the ideas may be a perfect fit for you. You may find yourself saying, "That's me. That's us! Hey, we can do this!" Other ideas may not fit and you may find yourself wanting to say: "I'll bet Wendy wouldn't have written that if she were married!" You can chalk those ideas up to the sweet dreams of a never-married woman if you want. But if there are some ideas that get you thinking about marriage and marital intimacy in a little different way, chalk those up to truths I've learned as I've immersed myself for more than twenty-five years in assisting couples and families to sort out and solve problems large and small.

SOME TRUTHS ABOUT TRUTH

Truths about intimacy can help clarify thoughts, feelings, and actions. These truths can strengthen your marriage whether yours is a vibrant, loving relationship; a marriage in the midst of an intimacy crisis; or a marriage where the two of you have drifted into feeling more like roommates or even strangers.

Truths about intimacy strengthen people and relationships. In addition to diminishing, and perhaps even eliminating, the frustration of spouses who are troubled about their sexual intimacy, these truths can also alleviate the anxiety of single people who are trying to "hang on" so they can one day enjoy true marital intimacy.

The more truths we understand about intimacy, the greater our desire and ability to be increasingly pure. The more pure we are, the greater our passion, and the greater our capacity to be truly intimate.

Purity and passion belong together.

They are eternal companions of intimacy.

And their friend is truth.

PART 1

AN INTRODUCTION TO INTIMACY

Thou shalt love thy neighbor as thyself.
—*D&C 59:6*

Chapter 1

UNDERSTANDING
INTIMACY

O f all the needs of the human heart, one of the greatest is our need for intimacy. We long to belong! We hunger to feel understood, thirst for companionship, yearn to commune. Our souls are enlarged when we experience deep caring and interpersonal connections that strengthen and sustain our hearts and minds. All relationships—with parents, children, spouses, grandparents, siblings, and friends—have the potential to be intimate, in terms of developing mutual feelings of trust and emotional closeness. In all of them, we can share precious thoughts and feelings. As we learn more about the incredible emotional and spiritual intimacy that can be part of all family relationships and friendships, we can better understand physical intimacy, that unique and grand intimacy sanctioned by God exclusively for husbands and wives.

What is intimacy? For some, an intimate moment was beautifully captured during the April 2001 general conference when

Sister Marjorie Hinckley, wife of the prophet, sang with the congregation and choir, "We Thank Thee, O God, for a Prophet." She seemed to be looking right at her husband as she sang along. Then when she sang the words, "and bask in its life-giving light," she just beamed!

Here are a few more "snapshots" of true intimacy:

• a husband curling his wife's hair and applying her makeup following her paralyzing stroke.

• a bone-weary young mother holding her son and her daughter on her lap, giving all she has to keep her children feeling safe, secure, loved, and happy.

• a sister persistently and prayerfully reaching out to her brother who has been choosing the road of immorality often traveled by those of the world.

• a mother and father standing with two of their children at the grave of their baby son, singing "Families Can Be Together Forever," and amid their sorrow feeling united as a family of five.

• a couple at their fiftieth wedding anniversary reflecting on the unanticipated joys and sorrows of their marriage and family life—complete with the heartaches of children's choices, health problems, and financial difficulties—and feeling more united than ever.

• a father in the delivery room gently cradling his moments-old newborn son and singing "The Spirit of God Like a Fire Is Burning."

• seven friends of varied ages sharing stories, laughter, and tears as they celebrate the seventieth birthday of one of them.

• a mother watching her adopted son joyfully swinging in the backyard and wishing his birth mother could share her moment of joy and gratitude.

• a grandfather taking his three-year-old granddaughter's hand and walking with her to the first parade of her life, and his first since his wife's death.

• a wife kindly but firmly speaking up for her husband in his absence when her family attacks his character.

• a young man making his girlfriend a sandwich and bringing

it to her office so she can use every minute to meet a major project deadline.

• a widow trying to figure out a problem and calling out: "John, what would *you* do?" as her relationship with her husband continues although he now lives on the other side of the veil.

• an engaged couple holding hands and looking deep into each other's eyes as they talk about the goals they have for their marriage.

• a husband giving his wife a priesthood blessing before she gives a talk.

• three daughters sitting on their elderly father's bed where he lies dying, holding his hands, smoothing his brow, and lovingly talking to him as he passes from this life into the next.

• a prophet praying on behalf of the Lord's people: "O Father . . ."

What are the common threads running through all of these intimate experiences? Closeness. Sharing. Caring. Trust. Traits such as these seem to be important parts of intimacy. Indeed, ongoing research has suggested that intimacy requires three things: reciprocal feelings of trust, emotional closeness, and the ability to openly communicate thoughts and feelings with another. (See G. M. Timmerman, "Concept Analysis of Intimacy," 19–30.) True intimacy for a covenant-making people also involves at least one more vital ingredient: the Spirit.

THE HOLY GHOST: THE TRUE RELATIONSHIP ENHANCER

The Holy Ghost can strengthen all relationships, and through His purifying and magnifying influence can and will enhance any couple's marital intimacy. How? Listen to what the Holy Ghost can do, as explained by Elder Parley P. Pratt:

"The gift of the Holy Ghost . . . quickens all the intellectual faculties, increases, enlarges, expands and purifies all the natural passions and affections, and adapts them, by the gift of wisdom, to their lawful use. It inspires, develops, cultivates, and matures all the fine-toned sympathies, joys, tastes, kindred feelings, and affections of our nature. It inspires virtue, kindness, goodness, tenderness, gentleness, and charity. It develops beauty of person, form, and features. It tends to health, vigor, animation, and social feeling. It invigorates all the faculties of the physical and intellectual man. It strengthens and gives tone to the nerves. In short, it is, as it were, marrow to the bone, joy to the heart, light to the eyes, music to the ears, and life to the whole being." (*Key to the Science of Theology*, 61.)

Thus, the Holy Ghost influences all our senses and strengthens us spiritually, emotionally, mentally, socially, and physically. Whatever level of intimacy we are presently capable of in our relationships, He can help us progress to a higher level as our abilities are expanded and purified through His influence.

Just think about how relationships are strengthened when the Spirit helps us to hear and see things about another that would otherwise go unnoticed by our mortal senses. We are able to hear the rest of the sentence that is lodged unspoken in the heart and mind of another.

When a child says, "Leave me alone," we are able to hear, "Please don't leave me alone." When a brother says, "I'm lonely," we can know those times when he's not missing others' company but is lonely for the best within himself. When an uncle says, "I'm just not celestial material," we can know how to respond when we are blessed by the Spirit to hear, "Please show me how I'm wrong to think I'm just not celestial material." When a mother says, "I'm so tired," we are able to hear, "I'm so tired of not being listened to, of not being taken seriously."

And the Spirit can help us to do the otherwise impossible. When a spouse pulls away from us, we can reach out again and again, rather than respond in kind or punish by withdrawing. When a friend refuses to forgive, we can forgive her or him. When a father looks angry, we can see his pain and speak to his hurt, rather than fruitlessly wrestle with his display of anger.

In these and numerous other ways, the Spirit of the Lord

helps us build intimate, loving relationships. Under the influence of the Holy Ghost we are able to live more impeccably the thirteenth Article of Faith, which is a relationship manual in itself. Imagine how our marriages, our families, and our friendships would blossom if this bedrock belief about purity were engraven upon our hearts and minds so that we were increasingly honest, true, chaste, benevolent, and virtuous; more able to do good to all men; more willing to believe all things, hope all things, and endure all things; and more eager to seek after everything that is virtuous, lovely, or of good report, or praiseworthy.

Think of the potential influence of this belief in our lives! If we really were honest, true, chaste, benevolent, and virtuous, we would be more able to do "good to all men" (including our family members), and to "believe all things" (especially that our family and friends love us and want the best for us). We would be able to "hope all things" (that our relationships can become an ever replenished and replenishing reservoir of love) so that we could "endure all things" (the sorrows, disappointments, and rigors of this life). Purity makes all these things possible.

If we *really* sought after only those things which are virtuous, lovely, or of good report or praiseworthy—in our thoughts and words about others and ourselves, and in our subsequent actions—we would abide in an abundance of love, intimacy, and passion that has been purified and enlarged through the influence of the Spirit. Caring, trust, and communication would come so much more easily to us. Clearly, purity is the key that unlocks the door to the kind of intimacy that brings forth new life in us and deep satisfaction to our souls.

PERSONAL PURITY AND INTIMACY

As women and men who strive to honor covenants we have made, we thrive on true intimacy—or intimacy as the Lord defines it. No illusions of intimacy will do. True intimacy is impossible to achieve in the absence of personal purity. Our capacity for intimacy is increased as we increase our personal purity, while decreased personal purity decreases our capacity for intimacy.

Intimacy flourishes in relationships that honor covenants. When we find ourselves in relationships that ignore or belittle our covenants, we are left bereft—and we wonder what is wrong with us. "Why can't we communicate better?" "Why doesn't he understand what I'm trying to say?" "Why doesn't she really care?" We wonder why all our best relationship efforts, even those the world would applaud, do not provide us with the palpable feelings we long for: of really being known by another, really being connected with someone, really mattering, really being loved.

Illusions of intimacy, lies about love, and distortions of passion are brought to us by Satan; true intimacy, genuine love, and pure passion are brought to us by the Spirit. And true intimacy that sustains spirit sons and daughters of heavenly parents is found within marriages, families, and friendships that involve the Savior.

OUR SAVIOR'S LOVE

Our ability to experience true intimacy of any kind in any relationship is directly related to how intimate our interactions are with the Lord. Truman Madsen said it well: "You cannot love until you are loved. You cannot be loved until you are Beloved, Beloved of God." (*Four Essays on Love,* 29.) President James E. Faust offered the plea for us to "not just . . . know about the Master, but to strive . . . to be one with Him." (see John 17:21) and to seek to "have a daily, personal relationship" with Him. (*Ensign,* January 1999, 2, 4.)

If we do not feel the love of the Savior in our lives, no other love can fill the void of being out of His presence. We lived with Him and with our heavenly parents before coming to this earth. What a gift it is to know that! What a heart-comforting thought it is to remember. No wonder we long for that feeling of true intimacy—over and over again. We come to this earth trailing our premortal memories of being immersed in the radiant light of His love!

A deep and abiding relationship with the Savior is indeed the only way to achieve true intimacy in our relationships with others. With the Savior's influence, our relationships have the power to sustain our heart and minds. With the Savior's touch, there is staying power to loving words and actions. With the Savior's tutoring, we have the ability to see beyond the obvious— to look deeper into the soul of another and to see the lovable, the redeemable, even the adorable.

The Savior has asked us to show our love for Him by keeping His commandments. (See John 14:15.) And as we are faithful and diligent in keeping His commandments, He promises to encircle us in the arms of His love. (See D&C 6:20.)

His showing His love to us in such an affectionate way— encircling us in the arms of His love—increases both our desire to keep His commandments and our ability to show our love to Him in the way that He has asked. And thus, this virtuous cycle gyroscopically spins, lifting us upward in our thoughts and feelings and actions, increasing our personal purity and bringing us closer to the Savior. Our closeness to the Savior fills us with His love, increasing our ability to love others and to feel love from others. Thus, the magnificent outcome of our drawing closer to the Savior is that He helps us to draw closer to everyone else.

A woman of great faith closed her eyes and described to her husband her feelings as she pictured herself being held by the Savior. "Brilliance!" she said. "More love than I've ever experienced in my life!" She instantly knew the feelings. Perhaps she was remembering.

The key to intimacy is personal purity!

So, if you long to belong, if you yearn for those heart-deep connections with others that will sustain your soul and carry you forward, increase the purity in your life by keeping the Lord's commandments. In fact:

If you want to be filled with the love of the Lord, keep His commandments.

If you want to feel loved, keep the Lord's commandments.

If you truly love someone and want to be able to communicate the depth of your feelings, keep the Lord's commandments.

And if you truly want to experience intimacy, any kind of intimacy, increase your personal purity by keeping the Lord's commandments.

Chapter 2

SIX TRUTHS
ABOUT LOVE

O h, I love that definition of love!" the young wife and mother said. "Tell me what it is one more time, slowly." A Chilean biologist's definition of love had caught her attention and spoken the intense feelings of her aching heart: "Love is opening space for the existence of another or acceptance of the other beside us in daily living" (H. R. Maturana, "Biology, Emotions and Culture.") That feeling of having space opened for her was exactly what this woman yearned to feel from her husband. She yearned to experience that he had room for her in his daily life, that in fact he wanted her and needed her.

During their first date, when he spoke only about himself, she felt invisible. On their honeymoon, when he worked on his graduate studies, she felt dismissed. And several years later, as she experienced him further immersing himself in his career and in his belief that he was right and she was wrong, she felt rejected and negated. She believed she was a complete nonentity in his life. Yet she loved him and wanted to feel love from him and to have him receive her love.

A popular song asked, "What's love got to do with it?" By contrast, a prophet proclaims that love is the answer. President Gordon B. Hinckley has stated that "there are good families everywhere, but there are too many who are in trouble. This is a malady with a cure. The prescription is simple and wonderfully effective. The answer is love." (*Ensign*, November 1997, 69.)

Some say that love is not enough. And sometimes it's not. "Love" is not enough when it is feigned or forced, demanded or commanded. "Love" is not enough when it is really lust. "Love" is not enough when it is really guilt or control. But love is always enough—and always will be enough and to spare—when it is really love.

Marital intimacy needs to be infused with and immersed in love. True love. Pure love. The kind of love Elder Howard W. Hunter spoke of when he said, "The pure love of Christ is the highest pinnacle the human soul can reach and the deepest expression of the human heart." (*That We Might Have Joy,* 170.) It is the kind of love poet laureate Maya Angelou described when she said, "I believe that it is love that heals." It is the kind of love respected theologian Truman G. Madsen distinguished from that of the world, which is love at first sight. "More accurately," said Dr. Madsen, "there is sight at first love," and while some may say that "'falling in love is sudden' . . . rising in love . . . is a lot more exciting. . . . But the rise is a slow, aching, anything-but-sudden process." (*Four Essays on Love,* 30.)

"Love is the very essence of life," President Hinckley said. "I am one who believes that love, like faith, is a gift of God." (*Ensign*, March 1984, 3.) Are we heeding these words of our prophet? Are we praying for this gift of God, this gift of the Spirit? Are we praying *for* love and *to* love? Are we heeding the marvelous words of Mormon to "pray unto the Father with all the energy of heart, that ye may be filled with this love"? (Moroni 7:48.) Are we praying to love as the Savior loves?

What happens when a wife fervently prays, "Please help me

to love my husband as the Savior loves him. Help me to see all that is good about him"? What occurs when a husband pleads with his Heavenly Father, "Help me to see my wife as Thou seest her. Help me to love her as Thou lovest her"? And perhaps there are times when the most effectual prayer of each spouse needs to be, "Please help me to see this situation from my spouse's point of view." Eyes that see things through a lens of love can see so much more clearly.

Because love is a gift of the Spirit, we need to do more than work for it; we need to pray for it. And because love is a gift from God, it follows that love will not be present in places where the Spirit of the Lord would not and cannot be. If we are breaking commandments within relationships and yet telling ourselves that we are "in love" or being loved or loving, we are being misled. However, when the Spirit is present, love is present. And reciprocally, when true love is present, the Spirit is present. They co-exist.

Hollywood typically portrays extramarital affairs as exciting, liberating, and love-drenched. And although there may be something that initially feels like excitement, freedom, and perhaps even "love," when covenants are being broken, it cannot be love. It is yet another illusion of the adversary himself. The Spirit cannot be present during extramarital affairs. So, if covenants and commandments are being broken, call it lust. Call it selfishness or shortsightedness. Call it momentary madness. But please don't call it love.

Mormon teaches us that true love, pure love, "suffereth long, and is kind, and envieth not, and is not puffed up, seeketh not her own, is not easily provoked, thinketh no evil, and rejoiceth not in iniquity but rejoiceth in the truth, beareth all things, believeth all things, hopeth all things, endureth all things." (Moroni 7:45.) What a litmus test for how loving we really are!

What can this kind of love do—this love that is kind, doesn't envy, isn't easily provoked, doesn't think evil, and rejoices in truth, this love that believes and hopes and endures? What difference does real love make? When love is present, it changes everything.

Eyes change, hearts change, attitudes and feelings change, cells change, souls change in the presence of love. One of our hymns speaks of love's influence: "There is beauty all around when there's love at home." (*Hymns,* no. 294.) The operative word is *when.* When love is not at home, it is difficult to recognize beauty anywhere, in anything, or in anyone, including ourselves.

LOVE AND HEALTH AND HEALING

Love is a biological dynamic with deep roots, according to Humberto Maturana, a Chilean biologist of some renown. As Latter-day Saints, we would add that love is a spiritual dynamic involving eons of premortal development. Talk about deep roots! Maturana also proffers the idea that "love is the most basic emotion for health and healing." Think of that. "The only thing that I know," he states, "is that love is a fundamental emotion in human beings," and that "most human diseases, most human suffering arise from interference with these fundamental emotions." (H. R. Maturana, "The Calgary-Chile Coupling," 9.) That's quite a statement from a biologist. Our diseases and suffering can arise from a lack of love!

Researchers J. Medalie and V. Goldbourt surveyed 10,000 men with heart disease. They found a 50 percent reduction in the frequency of chest pain in men who perceived that their wives were supportive and loving. ("Angina Predictors," 910–21.) Amazing! Physical and emotional symptoms actually diminish and often disappear when conflict is reduced and replaced with powerful, loving emotions.

Sometimes illness seems to strike out of the blue. But what if we were able to peer into our organs or cells and monitor the effects of our relationships and our life experiences? Would some illnesses catch us a little less by surprise?

Of course, diseases can just happen—some are hard wired. But could it be that our bodies are more likely to malfunction when we don't feel loved? John Gottman, renowned for his marital interaction research, found that women in ailing or failing marriages experienced increased infectious illnesses when their husbands showed a pattern of "stonewalling" or withdrawing from acknowledging or talking about their marital conflict. Gottman also found that as the marital interaction continued to deteriorate, the increasing distance, isolation, and loneliness had a negative effect on husbands' health as well. *(What Predicts Divorce?)*

Even our conversations do not go unnoticed by our cells. Have you noticed that? Have you ever had a conversation that helped you feel lighter, brighter? And conversely, have you had a conversation that gave you a headache?

One couple, Brian and Sarah, sought professional help to resolve long-standing marital conflict and resentment. Sarah, age thirty-five, was suffering with terminal cancer. Her wish, which Brian wanted to give her, was to resolve their marital issues before she died. As they showed love and caring to each other in ways and amounts that they never had before in their ten years of marriage, the change was almost miraculous. Sarah said, "I feel like these past few weeks have been very special. Brian has made a much bigger effort to listen." Brian was relieved that his wife was now believing and receiving his love. "A burden has been lifted," he said. One evening about three weeks into the process, the couple wrote down some things they appreciated about each other. They wrote about things they forgave each other for. They wrote about what they always wanted to honor about each other and about their marriage. They wrote a new love story about Sarah and Brian.

A few days later, Sarah died peacefully in Brian's arms.

How Can Spouses Show Love for Each Other?

If you wanted to increase by just 10 percent the love you show for your spouse, how would you "open space"—just a tithing's portion more space—for him or her in your life? Take a moment to really think about love as opening space for the existence of another, and see how brilliant you become about how to show more love to your spouse. Watch what happens to your relationship as you follow through on some of your ideas.

President Joseph F. Smith said, "Love in the family context is the glorious fulfillment of the life, atonement and death of Jesus Christ." (Truman G. Madsen, *Presidents of the Church,* tape 6.) How, then, can we increase love in our marriages and families? The bestselling books are "how-to" books. And the scriptures are the best of the "how-to" books, especially when it comes to love. Take First Nephi, for example. In that one book alone we can read about the shifts, failures, and renewals in various relationships: marital, parental, sibling, friend, in-law. In Moroni we have tender examples of father-son connections. And Third Nephi is packed with principles and practices that will enliven relationships. Let's consider a few.

SMALL VOICES PENETRATE

When the Nephites who had survived the tumult following Christ's death first heard the voice from heaven, "it was not a harsh voice, neither was it a loud voice. . . . it [was] a small voice [and] it did pierce them that did hear to the center." (3 Nephi 11:3.) One principle operating in marriages where love is felt is that small voices penetrate in positive ways. Spouses need to be careful not only about what they say but also about how they say it, meaning the tone and volume of their voices. Harsh, loud voices are emotionally and spiritually violent because they are usually fueled by a command, a demand, a position of "I'm right and you're wrong." Harsh, loud voices grieve life, they grieve the Spirit, and they shrink spouses' spirits. President Hinckley has even counseled us, "Let us lower our voices in our homes." (*Ensign,* November 2000, 89.)

When a spouse says, "I am so sorry," "I forgive you," "I love you," "I need you in my life," "I want to help you," "I'm scared," or "I've never been happier," the effect seems to be intensified when a small voice is used. Often the heart speaks most clearly in soft, low tones. The old saying really is true: "If you want to catch someone's attention, whisper."

Think of something you would most want to say to your spouse. Now think of saying it with a soft voice. Does the content of what you would say change, even just a bit? Would speaking with a softer, smaller voice clarify and fortify your message?

Now think of something you would most want to hear from your spouse—something that would lift your spirits, heal your heart, and lighten your load. Think of something that would let you know that your spouse has "opened space" for you in his or her life: space to be, space to offer your ideas, space to grow together. Hear in your mind's ear your spouse saying exactly the words you yearn to hear. Now hear them again, this time with a softer, lower tone. Does that voice "pierce your very soul" and "cause your heart to burn"?

President Hinckley has said that "quiet talk is the language of love. It is the language of peace. It is the language of God." (*Teachings of Gordon B. Hinckley,* 324–25.)

REPETITION REGISTERS TRUTH

A marvelous message about the need for and effect of repetition is offered in 3 Nephi 11:3–6. When the voice out of heaven came to the Nephites the first time, "it did pierce them that did hear it to the center." The voice affected the people physically and spiritually, causing their frames to quake and their hearts to burn. And yet, they didn't understand it. Even the second time they heard the voice, "they understood it not." It was only when they heard the voice the third time that they did "open their ears to hear it" and "they did understand the voice which they heard."

This is a great model for spouses as they interact with each other. Repetition of love can fill in emotional crevices, bridge spiritual gaps, and melt down formerly impenetrable walls. One wife found that wonderful things happened when she didn't hold back on saying to her husband, "I believe in you. I trust you." Initially, she had felt the truth of these words predominantly because of her abiding faith in the power of Christ's atonement—that is, she believed in her husband because she had faith in the Savior. Then, through various experiences in scripture study, prayer, priesthood blessings, fasting, and temple worship, she came to believe more and more in her husband, and her trust in him grew. She found that as she expressed her heartfelt sentiment to him over and over again, his confidence began to wax strong.

Another wife, after two years of marriage, had convinced herself and almost convinced her husband that she just didn't have what it took for a great marriage relationship. She had threatened to end their marriage almost from the beginning and was easily discouraged over any disagreement or difficulty they had. To her, conflict was evidence of her failure as a woman worthy of love and capable of loving. A major turning point occurred when her husband began relentlessly expressing his love to her. First thing in the morning, last thing at night, and several times during the day, he told her how he adored her, missed her, and couldn't believe how fortunate he was to be married to her. Her reaction was similar to that of the Nephites. Initially, his words pierced her soul, but she couldn't really understand them. She would often say to him, "I don't understand why you love me. No one else ever has."

However, through his patient and consistent expressions of love—both showing and saying—she shifted, just as the Nephites had done, from "not understanding," to opening her ears to hear his words, to "looking steadfastly" toward him and their marriage.

Spouses need to be persistent in offering and showing love to each other. Again the Savior sets the example. In 3 Nephi 9:13–21, we see how many ways the Lord offers to help us, how many ways he pleads, "Return unto me," "Come unto me." When spouses follow the Savior's example, repeatedly entreating each other to come closer, marvelous things happen. Space is opened, even space that has been closed for years—and seemingly hermetically sealed! Repetition breaks the seal.

Repetition helps to register truth. Remember, it was not until the third time that the Nephites understood the voice they had heard twice before. If your spouse doesn't always respond to your offerings of love the first time, don't take it as a personal affront. Try it a second time. Try it a third time. Repetition of true love is good for all involved.

Actually, we may ask if there really is such a thing as repetition. We are always changing. The second time we hear something we have new ears—ears that are different because of what they heard the first time and because of intervening experiences. The repetition changes us, just as the initial sound did. With each repetition we hear something different because we are changed by each experience of a sound, sight, or touch.

Think about the temple and the repetition we hear there. Think about how we continually see or hear things in a new way in our temple worship because intervening experiences have changed us. The temple ceremony hasn't changed, but because we have, the ceremony is never the same.

Think about the scriptures. We can never really say, "I've finished reading the Book of Mormon." Every time we read it, it's new. As we read by the light of the Spirit, truths that have been hidden to us are suddenly highlighted on our pages—even those pages we've read many times before and marked with our manmade highlighters.

Think about words and deeds. Saying "I love you" in word and in deed never gets old when it is heart-felt. Hearing a sincere "I love you" never gets old. Hearing a genuine "I am so sorry" never gets old. Repetition is good for each person's soul. And the repetition of real love in word and in deed creates a greater intimacy between spouses.

COMMENDATIONS ARE CRUCIAL

In the Doctrine and Covenants, the Lord tells us, "Strengthen your brethren in all your conversation, in all your prayers, in all your exhortations, and in all your doings." (D&C 108:7.) One sure way to show love for your spouse is through commendations—positive, heartfelt comments about your loved one and his or her abilities. In 3 Nephi 11:7 Heavenly Father sets the example for us as He introduces the Savior to the Nephites: "Behold my Beloved Son, in whom I am well pleased." In that one statement, God the Father does at least three things:

1. He publicly establishes His relationship with His Son.
2. He publicly expresses love for His Son.
3. He publicly commends His Son.

What can we learn from that one sterling comment? First, we can understand the importance of establishing our relationships with loved ones in the presence of others. Many couples feel most like "a couple" when they are with other people. Using "we" language in public establishes the relationship for the spouses themselves as well as for others. These words draw a boundary around them as a couple.

If you and your spouse are doubting your "couplehood"—not feeling very "coupled" or connected—try talking about "us" and "we" and "our" just a bit more around other people and see what happens. The presence of witnesses is important, and not just at a wedding ceremony. The credible message that you and your spouse are a team will start being heard—most importantly, by each of you.

Think again of the wonderful statement "Behold my Beloved Son, in whom I am well pleased." If every time you introduced your spouse to someone, you expressed your love and offered some positive comment about him or her, what effect would that have on your relationship? Talk about "opening space"! Can you imagine how that introduction would breathe life into your marriage? Offer a commendation about your spouse publicly and watch the changes—in your spouse, in your relationship, and even in yourself.

The best-kept secret in many marriages is the strengths spouses see in each other. Imagine if they had hidden video cameras and a husband could hear and see his wife speaking about him to her friend, saying that he was more than she had ever hoped for; or picture a wife hearing her husband say to his colleague that he would marry her all over again, just as she is today. What difference do you think that would make in the way they showed their love for each other—and received each other's love? Surely they would open even more space in their lives for each other!

And now a caution. As powerful and useful as public commendations are, if the only time spouses hear how much they are loved is publicly—for example, during testimony meeting—the commendations will probably fall on deaf ears. One woman said, "I always try to tell my children that I love my husband." Her listener replied, "Did you tell them with about as much enthusiasm as you just now told me? If so, your children and your husband probably haven't ever believed it!"

The First Four Minutes of Contact. How could this woman really show and speak her love for her husband so that he would experience and believe her love? One pair of researchers found that as the first four minutes of contact between a couple goes, so goes the relationship. (Zunin and Zunin, *Contact: The First Four Minutes.*) This suggests that another key to opening space and showing love is to have every "first four minutes" of contact be positive. For example, the first four minutes in the morning between you and your spouse need to be positive, loving moments. Set the alarm four minutes early—even on hectic days. Just four minutes of showing love, encouraging each other's success for the day, hugging—even slipping into the lost art of morning smiling—will bring amazing results. The same is true for the next "first four minutes" during the day that a couple are together. Those next "first four minutes" may be in the evening when they arrive home from their various activities of the day.

The first four minutes of contact are *not* the time to say "Why didn't you . . . ?" or "Why can't you ever . . . ?" Save those for the fifth minute. The first four minutes are for engaging with each other, expressing how glad you are to see each other, remembering and celebrating your love for each other. Just four minutes of showing and sharing love will make all the difference to how the discussions, decisions, and duties during the fifth, sixth, and twentieth minutes go. Over time, as you experience four minutes of positive interaction during each "new" contact between you and your spouse, you will open more and more space for each other, and love will grow.

One couple found that positive changes in their marital intimacy naturally started to occur when they shared a "ten-second kiss" during their first four minutes of contact. Initially, they literally clocked their lip embrace. Ten seconds was longer than they thought! But they soon discovered the benefits. Their ten-second kisses started to help them come out of the world and into "their" world. Their ten-second kisses started to change what they talked about during their first four minutes of contact, and soon neither ten seconds nor four minutes was time enough to share with each other their love, admiration, dedication, and devotion.

The 5:1 Ratio. Researchers have become very interested in determining the ratio of positive to negative communication between spouses that will keep a marriage on a pathway of improvement and increased happiness. The magic ratio they have found is five to one. That is, as long as there is at least five times more affection, humor, smiling, complimenting, agreement, empathy, and active listening than there is criticism and disagreement, your marriage will prosper. (See Gottman and Silver, *Why Marriages Succeed or Fail.*) What does the ratio in your marriage look like? Again, repetition and consistency are important. Having a five-to-one ratio of positive to negative communication only on Sundays will not strengthen your marriage through the rest of the week—let alone through the rest of your lives.

How can you start improving the ratio of positive to negative communication in your marriage? An interesting fact about commending your spouse is that the more you do it, the more you see in him or her to commend. Why is this so? Because in order to commend, you really need to study a situation. This is no place for fluffy, superficial comments; it's time to get up close and personal! You need to look closely, to really *notice*, in order to commend your spouse's goodness, competence, courage, tenacity, and patience—perhaps even his or her patience with you! As you work harder at being a "strength detective," your interactions will change, you'll uncover even more things to commend in your spouse, and your positive to negative ratio will change. It's no wonder that marriages start building naturally and securely within such a commendation-dominated environment.

What is another effect of these sincere, positive comments? Commendations seem to naturally decrease condemnations. The tendency to point out your spouse's flaws and failures begins to wane as you focus on his or her strengths. In this way the 5:1 ratio of positive to negative communication also becomes easier to achieve. And over time, the positive to negative ratio tends to improve even further.

Love Grows When It Is Believed and Received

In 3 Nephi 10:4–6, over and over again we read the Savior's words offering His help: "How oft have I gathered you," "How oft would I have gathered you," and "How oft will I gather you." He offers us His gift of love many times, and He tells us that far too often His gift of helping and healing has been rejected: "And ye would not."

Do you know the feeling of offering a gift of love to your spouse and not having it received? Do you sometimes feel that you have more love to give than your spouse has the ability or desire to receive? Spouses feel neglected and even rejected when their desire to help their partners isn't accepted. Conversely, wonderful things can happen in relationships when gifts of love are believed and received.

Many times in marriages, a gift of love is not received because it is not seen as a gift. Often the gift of love offered to solve a problem or help a spouse is perceived by that spouse as just adding to the problem—or even as the problem itself. What happens to your perception about your spouse's disappointing or even annoying behavior when you consider this question: "If I were to believe that this is my spouse's best effort to help solve our problems so that we can build our relationship, how would I respond? Would it increase my ability to believe and receive my spouse's love?"

One husband was upset when his gift to his grieving wife was rejected. Her father had recently died, and her husband offered to take her on a short vacation. For him, it was his best effort to "gather her" and to comfort her, but she experienced his idea as negating her pain, and she "would not." This experience made each of their beliefs about the other more rigid and unyielding. He believed, "Nothing I do makes a difference." She believed, "He really doesn't care about me."

Several weeks after this grave misunderstanding, they opened their hearts to each other. They discovered that the thing he longed for most from her was to feel appreciated. And the desire of her heart was to feel that she had a major place in his—to feel loved and cared for by him. The husband apologized for his ineptness in not giving his wife what she needed the most at this tender time in her life. He expressed his deep desire to give her all the space she needed to grieve. He was surprised and delighted to learn that the space she needed—in fact, longed for—was to be right next to him! The wife apologized for not believing and receiving her husband's gift. She expressed, in a different manner than ever before, how important he was to her, how powerful his influence was in her life, how vital his view of her was.

Sometimes a spouse's gift of love is the expression of his or her hurting heart, concerns, and worries. Have you had the experience of expressing a concern to your spouse, only to have him or her say, "Oh, that's nothing to worry about." How did you feel? When our words, concerns, or commendations are downplayed or negated, *we* feel negated.

By contrast, the Savior set the example of always being willing to hear, and to heal, our suffering and our pains. He never dismisses or negates our longings or our love. As spouses follow Christ's example, believing and receiving the various gifts He offers and that each spouse offers, the love they experience with each other will be magnified and magnificent!

An important way to believe and receive your spouse's love, to open space for him or her in your life, is to be responsive to his or her desires to be with you. In Third Nephi, when the Savior was ready to leave the Nephites, He realized that they needed him to stay, and He said, in effect, "I perceive that you don't want me to go, so I'll stay." Some people are so busy managing their time that their marriages are suffering. Can you imagine what would happen if you said to your spouse, "I was supposed to be doing (such and such), but I can tell we need more time together, so I'll stay here with you and rearrange that commitment." What a message of love!

PURE TOUCH TESTIFIES OF LOVE

In 3 Nephi 11:14 we read that the Savior invited the people to "arise and come forth unto me, that ye may thrust your hands into my side, and also that ye may feel the prints of the nails in my hands and in my feet, that ye may know that I am the God of Israel, and the God of the whole earth, and have been slain for the sins of the world." The Savior's desire to have them come physically close and touch His side and hands and feet was another witness of His love for them. And reciprocally, the people's desire to come close enough to touch Him demonstrated their love for Him. Both the giving and receiving of pure, tender touch testifies of love.

There may be times when the presence of others as witnesses magnifies the testifying influence of a spouse's tender touch. When one wife was asked, "What is the smallest amount of change that would tell you that you and your husband are making progress in your marriage?" she wept as she answered, "If he would put his arm around me during sacrament meeting." Another husband was asked what his wife did that let him know she really loved him. He responded, "She hugs me in front of the kids."

The tender touch of a spouse's hand can provide evidence that you are loved, that you are not alone, that he or she really does care and wants to be there for you. One wife said, "I really feel my husband's love when he tenderly puts his hands on both of my shoulders and talks with me eye to eye." A husband said, "I feel an extra level of comfort when my wife hugs me—actually, it feels more like she holds me—with one of her hands at the back of my neck and her other hand at the back of my waist." Being physically "in touch" with one another can increase feelings of being emotionally and mentally and spiritually in touch.

Think of a conversation you would most want to have with your spouse. Think of the words you would want to say and hear. Now imagine having that same conversation in the presence of pure, testifying touch. Does it change what you want to say? Is your ability to speak from your heart increased? Does it change what you want to hear? Is your ability to hear with your heart increased when tender touch is added?

Owning Our Part Helps Us Overcome Problems

In 3 Nephi 14:3, the Lord says, "Why beholdest thou the mote that is in thy brother's eye, but considerest not the beam that is in thine own eye?" Normally, both spouses contribute to problems within marriages. It is seldom useful to point out how your spouse is to blame for those problems. Rather, a more fruitful question is: "What am I doing (wittingly or unwittingly) that

keeps the problem going?" ("What is the beam in my eye?")
Motes and beams fit together into vicious cycles that start to have
lives of their own. If you've ever thought to yourself: "Here we go
again," just after vowing never to say or do something again, you
know the power of a vicious cycle.

A classic example of a vicious cycle in which couples can
become trapped is the nag-withdraw cycle. The more she nags, the
more he withdraws; the more he withdraws, the more she nags. If
a wife is concerned about her husband's withdrawing, his "mote"
(withdrawing) is both a response to, and a trigger for, her "beam"
(nagging—also known as repetitive encouragement!). And
reciprocally, her nagging (her "beam") is both a response to, and a
trigger for, her husband's withdrawing (his "mote"). His mote
invites her beam, and her beam invites his mote. Both keep the
vicious cycle of the problem going around and around.

Cycles can be portrayed as having six elements: the thoughts,

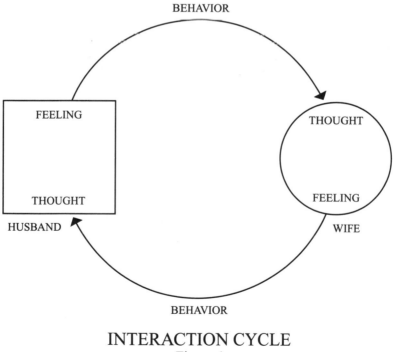

INTERACTION CYCLE
Figure 1

feelings, and behavior of each spouse. (See Tomm, "Towards a Cybernetic-Systems Approach to Family Therapy.") Figure 1 illustrates these six elements in the cycle.

When trying to understand the interaction of the various parts of a vicious cycle, we can begin with any one of the six elements. Arbitrarily, let's begin with the wife's behavior, her nagging. Nagging can sound like: "Why don't you come home earlier?" "Why don't you ever help out with the kids?" "Why does your work always come first?" Her husband hears her words and may think: "Nothing I do makes her happy. Why bother? Unless I do it her way, it's never good enough. She's trying to control me." He may feel guilty, discouraged, frustrated, or inadequate. In an effort to "keep the peace," he may withdraw—into silence, into his work, into activities outside their home.

When his wife sees him being less available to her and their family, showing less affection, or saying less to her when he is

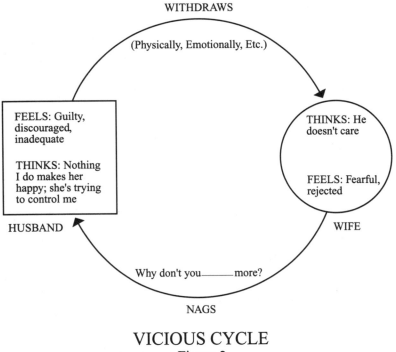

VICIOUS CYCLE
Figure 2

home, she may tell herself, "He doesn't care about me or about our marriage and family. What am I going to do?" She may feel fearful, rejected, and worried. In an effort to get her husband more involved in her life and in their marriage and family, she may pursue him more. From her point of view she is trying to invite him back home. However, he experiences her behavior as nagging and as pointing out, yet again, how inadequate he is . . . and thus the cycle continues viciously. (See figure 2.)

The good news is that a vicious cycle can begin to shift into a *virtuous* cycle if we change any one of the six parts. A change in one part of the cycle affects every other part. It really is true that "out of small things proceedeth that which is great" (D&C 64:33) and "a very large ship is benefited very much by a very small helm in the time of a storm" (D&C 123:16).

So how can this husband and wife shift their vicious cycle into a virtuous cycle? The Savior tells us how to approach these situations. He counsels us to stop trying to solve the problem by trying to get the other person to change. Rather, we should take ownership for our part. The Lord said: "How wilt thou say to thy brother: Let me pull the mote out of thine eye—and behold, a beam is in thine own eye." (3 Nephi 14:4.)

Then the Savior tells us where to start solving the problem: "First cast the beam out of thine own eye." (3 Nephi 14:5.) He wants us to take ownership not just by acknowledging our part in the problem but by changing our behavior—first! He wants us to *do something different*. It isn't enough for the wife to say, "Oh, I know I probably get after my husband too much and don't show enough appreciation for what he does." The Savior wants her to cast her beam out—to stop nagging and start showing appreciation. And it's not enough for the husband to say, "I know that I don't talk enough to my wife or spend enough time helping out at home." The Savior wants him to cast his own beam out, to start talking and helping more.

Let's consider how a virtuous cycle unfolded when the husband in our example first cast out his beam. When he realized his part in their vicious cycle and learned how his wife was feeling because of his withdrawing behavior, he started to come home a little earlier and to ask her, "How was your day?" Once a week he also phoned her unexpectedly during the day from work and asked if there was anything he could do to help her when he came home that evening.

His small changes started to catch his wife's attention, and she began to believe: "Well, maybe he really does care. Maybe he really does want to be with me." She started feeling cared for and loved. She relaxed, reduced her worrying, and started feeling safe. When that happened, she started to be able to see more clearly all the good things her husband was already doing. She started showing appreciation and love for her husband. Over time she actually started to suggest that he enjoy some fishing or basketball as a way of unwinding from the intensity of his work.

And what was the effect of her new behavior? Her husband

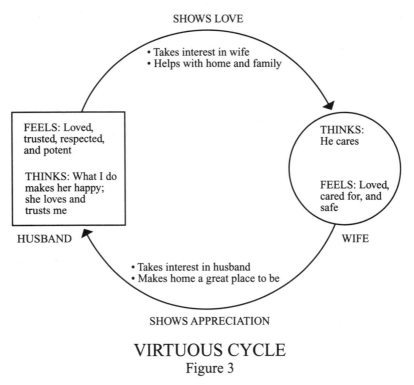

SHOWS LOVE

- Takes interest in wife
- Helps with home and family

FEELS: Loved, trusted, respected, and potent

THINKS: What I do makes her happy; she loves and trusts me

HUSBAND

THINKS: He cares

FEELS: Loved, cared for, and safe

WIFE

- Takes interest in husband
- Makes home a great place to be

SHOWS APPRECIATION

VIRTUOUS CYCLE
Figure 3

started to think, "She really does appreciate what I do. She loves me, trusts me, and wants me to be happy. And she understands all I am trying to do for the family." His feelings of being loved, appreciated, and trusted also helped him feel potent and powerful for the first time in their marriage. He started to think of even more ways to show love to his wife and be involved in their marriage and family. He started to take her fishing with him and to jog with her after work rather than playing basketball with his friends, because he really wanted to be with *her*. In this way a virtuous cycle of love, appreciation, trust, and increased communication continued. (See figure 3.)

Owning our part in problems increases our ability to find solutions. Because spouses' thoughts, feelings, and behaviors are so intertwined, amazing changes can occur when spouses first cast out their own beams.

President Brigham Young's counsel to women (which is equally valid for men) speaks to the power of this principle: "Were I a woman possessed of great powers of mind, filled with wisdom, and upon the whole, a magnanimous woman, and had been privileged with my choice, and had married a man, . . . he not answering my expectations, and I being sorry that I had made such a choice, let me show my wisdom by not complaining about it. . . . By seeking to cast off her husband—by withdrawing her confidence and good will from him, she casts a dark shade upon his path, when, by pursuing a proper course of love, obedience, and encouragement, he might attain to that perfection she had anticipated in him." (*Discourses of Brigham Young,* 202.)

A QUESTION TO CONSIDER

Which of the six truths from Third Nephi discussed in this chapter could best help you and your spouse strengthen your marriage?

1. Small voices penetrate.
2. Repetition registers truth.

3. Commendations are crucial.
4. Love grows when it is believed and received.
5. Pure touch testifies of love.
6. Owning our part helps us overcome problems.

PART 2

OBSTACLES TO INTIMACY

Like weeds and rocks that prevent growth in a garden, obstacles often exist in the intimate relationships between husbands and wives. These obstacles keep spouses from fully embracing each other or accepting further truths about intimacy.

Three threats to marital intimacy are
- *personal impurity,*
- *worldly views of love, and*
- *anger.*

Chapter 3

THE DEVASTATION
OF IMPURITY

If there is anything gross, defiling, of an illicit nature, obscene, or unclean, the adversary entices us to seek after these things. And he seeks to convince us that such things are normal, healthy, and good. His desire is to dissuade us from seeking virtue and to persuade us to be impure. Why? Because *impurity impedes intimacy.* The adversary will never experience intimacy, and he doesn't want us to either. He will never enjoy a marriage and family, or have true friends. Thus, in an effort to make us miserable like he is (see 2 Nephi 2:27), his goal is to keep us from building relationships that will sustain us throughout eternity.

There are so many ways to be personally impure, as King Benjamin explained: "I cannot tell you all the things whereby ye may commit sin; for there are divers ways and means, even so many that I cannot number them." (Mosiah 4:29.) However, there are some things we do know about sin and about personal impurity:

- Impurity decreases marital intimacy.
- Impurity never brings happiness.
- Impurity has highly predictable consequences.
- Impurity decreases our ability to understand and remember truth.

IMPURITY DECREASES MARITAL INTIMACY

Let's start with the bottom line: Sin and sexual intimacy in its most fulfilling form do not, and cannot, go together. While some people may equate the two, nothing could be further from the truth.

Personal impurity of any kind—lying, cheating, stealing, or viewing or doing anything that makes the Spirit flee—hinders and impedes true intimacy. Marital intimacy as the Lord intended it remains out of reach for those trying to cover up present or past unrepented sins. Impurity leads to deceit and illusion, making honest communication impossible. In short, sin eventually pulls people apart. Always.

The kind of physical intimacy sanctioned by God, which brings a closeness beyond anything this world dreams of, is possible only within the bounds of marriage and can be partaken of only by spouses who are striving to be pure. Any other physical "intimacies" are outside of God's law and, therefore, can never bring real love and true intimacy. All such illicit sexual relationships are deadly—to love, to the spirits of those involved, and to their relationships.

Some people are constrained from enjoying marital intimacy because they feel impure, through no fault of their own but because they are burdened by the weight of the "sins of this generation" and the "sins of their fathers." One such woman was spiritually dead after participating in an extramarital affair. A friend attempted to resuscitate her spirit by asking, "When did you first start believing that you were unworthy, unclean, and 'just not celestial material'?" The woman realized that she had started betraying herself when she was very young. She believed she was unclean because of the contaminating sexual abuse experiences she had been forced to participate in and observe as an innocent child.

All her life, this wounded woman had believed that *she* must be "evil," "black," and "dark" because of the abuse perpetrated against her. This erroneous belief led, in a way difficult to understand by those who have not experienced sexual abuse, to her involvement in further illicit sexual experiences and prevented her from enjoying physical intimacy with her spouse.

Personal impurity breeds personal impurity from generation to generation unless stopped by the truth and power of the Atonement. In 2 Nephi 25:12 we learn of three things that make it difficult to believe and receive the Savior: iniquity, hard hearts, and stiff necks. These same three things—all close associates of personal impurity—prevent husbands and wives from believing and receiving each other's love as well as believing and receiving the healing power and love available through the Atonement.

Pervading, intrusive influences of personal impurity were evident in the marriage of one couple who were avid swimmers. They were trying to reclaim their marital intimacy but felt as if they were "swimming upstream" against obstacles created by their past behaviors. A friend offered them this metaphor: "The two of you are the fortunate owners of a pool—a marital intimacy pool that can refresh and invigorate, soothe and relax. This is a pool in which you can grow as a couple and in which each of you can grow into even more of who you are as a man and as a woman. However, there is a problem with your pool: It is contaminated.

"Because of your premarital immorality, pre- and post-marital exposures to pornography, and an extramarital affair, your pool has become a cesspool. It is contaminated with lust and rejection. To put even your little toe into such a pool is to become contaminated with lustful feelings and feelings of rejection."

Turning to the wife, the friend said, "You are exquisitely sensitive to the lustful feelings in the pool and withdraw from your husband when you sense these." Turning to the husband, she said, "You are exquisitely sensitive to the feelings of rejection in the pool and withdraw from your wife when you sense these."

Then the friend said to the couple, "You've each made some weak efforts to clean out your pool. You've stretched a little netting on top of the water to take off the floaters—that is, you've stopped some of your overt behaviors related to pornography—but the real grime of lust is still in the pool. You've tried a little chlorine, consisting of a few apologies to clean up both the lust and the rejection. But that has not been enough. Something dramatic needs to happen now. Your marital intimacy pool needs to be thoroughly drained—cleansed from all the rejection and all the lust—and then filled with pure, clean water. Removing all the impurities by removing all the contaminated water is the only solution at this point. Only then can pure water be added. This will happen only with much work on both of your parts. It will involve major changes in your thoughts, feelings, and behaviors, and working with the Lord in a way neither of you has done before. The Savior is the source of power to drain the contaminated water, and He is the source of living, pure water. His pure, living water will bring you the joyful, loving, and healing experiences that will cleanse, refresh, and buoy you up as a couple."

The couple diligently sought in every way they could to come out of the world and to come closer to the Savior than they ever had before. Through these relentless efforts they began to feel the healing and hallowing blessings of the Atonement in their marriage. And their marital cesspool was transformed into a life- and love-generating marital intimacy pool.

IMPURITY NEVER BRINGS HAPPINESS

The happiest place on earth is never the heart or mind of an immoral man or woman. Satan's great lie is that sin will make you happy. The truth is that you can never sin enough to make you happy. The momentary pleasures of sin are sooner or later followed by anguish and suffering. An ancient prophet grieving about his son's immorality lamented, "Wickedness never was happiness." (Alma 41:10.) And centuries later a latter-day prophet, President Ezra Taft Benson, echoed the same sentiment: "There is no lasting happiness in immorality. There is no joy to be found in breaking the law of chastity." ("The Law of Chastity," 51.)

As with other sacred experiences ordained by God, there are laws that govern sexual intimacy. Indeed, there are "law[s] irrevocably decreed . . . before the foundations of this world, upon which all blessings are predicated." (D&C 130:20.) To receive the blessings associated with marital intimacy, we need to live the laws upon which those blessings are predicated. We can't have it both ways. We can't break those laws and then murmur and wonder why we don't receive the blessings.

Extramarital sex, masturbation, homosexual activities, and many other sexual practices condoned by the world break the eternal laws upon which the blessings of marital intimacy are predicated. Marital intimacy is not possible when these activities are part of either or both partners' lives. Sex is possible. Short-lived, hot-blooded hormonal rushes are possible. But physical intimacy that shores up each spouse, breathes life into each spouse and into their relationship, and sustains them through their joys and sorrows—that kind of intimacy is only possible when eternal laws are kept.

There seems to be a perpetually escalating contest to see just how much distortion and perversion about love and sex can be introduced into the human mind without protest. Through the world's media, we as a society absorb and adapt to the lies of

Lucifer more and more quickly. And it shows—in our behavior, thoughts, and feelings. It often seems that the only reason these days that we walk out of a movie—which a few years ago we would have never gone to see—is to go to the kitchen for a drink of water! The off-putting movies from the big screen are now playing on a television screen near you.

While "the whole world lieth in sin, and groaneth under darkness and under the bondage of sin" (D&C 84:49), we, as men and women of covenant, have been given more light and knowledge than the world. So, when we as Latter-day Saints subscribe to lies about love and sex, we're in much more trouble than the world is. Men and women of the world who break the Lord's commandments have at least not broken covenants. Therefore, the world's groans are whispers compared to the cries of men and women who have broken their covenants, and who in the light of day realize what they have done.

When Latter-day Saints sin against the greater light, the ensuing darkness is so much greater. The permutations and combinations of unhappiness brought into their lives and the lives of those they love are phenomenally heart-breaking. The Lord meant it when He said, "Of him unto whom much is given much is required; and he who sins against the greater light shall receive the greater condemnation." (D&C 82:3.) Once we have received the gift of the Holy Ghost, experienced His companionship, and made sacred covenants with the Lord, we "can't sin so cheap no more," as President Heber C. Kimball once said. (*1844 Journal.*)

One couple of covenant believed that their relationship was lacking something. They felt disconnected from each other. They were discouraged in their efforts—minimal and erratic though they had been—to have the kind of marital intimacy they hoped to have. Each was on the verge of saying, "If this is marriage, I don't want it for eternity!" One spouse offered a world-drenched idea of how to "spice up" their sexual relationship. The outcome? The "spice" opened wide the door for the adversary to wreak havoc with their marriage. They almost lost their relationship, their direction in life, and their sense of who—and whose—they really are.

Perhaps the greatest tragedy of all is that there was no need for this couple to look to the world for "spice." The good news is that there is *more* excitement, *more* delight, *more* joy, *more* love, *more* fun, *more* sweetness, and *more* savor waiting right around the corner through increased obedience to the laws of God—especially when a couple chooses to turn that corner together. As this couple incorporated gospel insights and truths about intimacy into their marriage, the "spice" of the world paled, even seeming pathetic, next to the blessings that flowed from true sexual intimacy.

IMPURITY HAS HIGHLY PREDICTABLE CONSEQUENCES

The consequences of sin are, sadly, highly predictable. There are few surprises in a life that is under the influence of the adversary. As an example, research has now shown that if a dating couple would like to lessen their chances for their relationship to be a long-term success, all they have to do is have premarital sexual experiences! (See Jeffry H. Larson, *Should We Stay Together?*) And if you want to undermine your feelings of self-worth and ensure that guilt and shame will be your constant companions—assuming you are not past feeling—all you have to do is participate in any sexual experience prohibited by the Lord.

Another predictable and tragic consequence is that sin makes us stupid. It delays our spiritual, mental, social, and emotional growth and development. And sin costs a lot, too! It is costly in so many ways—financially, emotionally, spiritually, socially, mentally, and physically. It's no wonder that sin and its consequences are the most stressful elements of life.

The consequences of impurity are so predictable that we could begin listing them alphabetically: abuse, betrayal, cruelty, deceit, envy, fear, guilt, humiliation, and so on. We could expand our ability to predict the consequences of sin by drawing a series of concentric circles to show who actually pays those consequences: self, family, friends, work, church, community, nation, and so on. And we could further add to the list of consequences by considering the innumerable positive life experiences an impure person will miss out on, such as joy, love, cheer, freedom, security, confidence, and peace.

Prophets and apostles have warned us about the grievous outcomes of sin. President Joseph F. Smith declared, "Secret sins [will] bring not only physical punishment, but sure spiritual death. You cannot hide the penalty which God has affixed to them. . . . It is the loss of self-respect, it is physical debility, it is insanity, indifference to all powers that are good and noble—all these follow in the wake of the sinner in secret, and of the unchaste. Unchastity, furthermore, not only fixes its penalty on the one who transgresses, but reaches out unerring punishment to the third and fourth generation, making not only the transgressor a wreck, but mayhap involving scores of people in his direct line of relationship, disrupting family ties, breaking the hearts of parents, and causing a black stream of sorrow to overwhelm their lives." (*Gospel Doctrine*, 335.)

Other consequences to breaking the seventh commandment have been pointed out in Elder Neal A. Maxwell's statement about society's responses: "Some of the sad consequences . . . are: penicillin instead of abstinence; pills instead of children; transient partners instead of marriage; childbirth with unwed parents; old perversions masquerading as new thrills—and all of it soaked in alcohol." (*Notwithstanding My Weakness*, 103.)

IMPURITY DECREASES OUR ABILITY TO UNDERSTAND AND REMEMBER TRUTH

Our ability to hear, understand, remember, and resonate to truth is commensurate with our level of personal purity. Purity brings clarity of thought; impurity brings confusion. Purity keeps our eyes open and our ears unstopped. Impurity blinds us to our blindness and silences the trumpeting of truth that surrounds us. At best, we hear a cacophony of sounds; at worst, nothing at all.

At birth a veil is drawn over our premortal memories, and yet when we hear truth we recognize it. Truth stirs something within us. One of the saddest consequences of impurity is that a sin-immersed person no longer resonates to truth—in fact, that person will doubt truth, calling the bearers of truth "liars," "naive," and "out of touch." Elder Bruce R. McConkie spoke of the effect of adultery upon one's spirit: "Adultery so dulls the spiritual sensitivities of men [and women] that it becomes exceedingly hard for them to believe the truth when they hear it." (*The Mortal Messiah*, 2:225.)

Our responses to truth are a reflection of our present spiritual state. One couple read an article on truths about marital intimacy together. The wife savored every word. The husband, whose spirit was still reeling from the consequences of adultery, said that he "really didn't get it." Impurity and an impairment of intellectual abilities often correlate.

Under the influence of sin and wickedness, hearts are hardened, minds are darkened, and eyes are blinded. (See 1 Nephi 12:17.) When truth is offered, it bounces right off. Impurity even decreases our ability to experience the truthfulness of someone's love for us. When we are blinded by the adversary or our own insecurities and unresolved past issues, someone may offer us pure, steady, resilient love, but we may not be able to see it, believe it, or receive it. We may be like the people described in Acts 28:26–27: "Hearing ye shall hear, and shall not understand; and seeing ye shall see, and not perceive. For the heart of this people is waxed gross, and their ears are dull of hearing, and their eyes have they closed."

Impurity decreases our ability not only to be sensitive to truth but also to understand the feelings of others. "I never knew that was how my spouse was feeling" is an all-too-common response of those steeped in impurity. The ability to take a wider look at the world is lost. Peripheral vision—to see what's happening with others on the sidelines of life—is obscured. Myopia takes over. "If it affects my well-being, it's important; if not, I'm not interested" becomes the stance of the personally impure person—a dramatic contrast to the Spirit-influenced heart and mind that are naturally concerned for the well-being of others.

Impurity diminishes our ability to draw distinctions between right and wrong. Subtlety is lost on the personally impure. Since people who are impure are in darkness, it takes dramatic differences between black and white to catch their attention. Often, they've been so immersed in blatantly seductive practices that only the most monumental distinctions register with them. Wake-up calls are often needed. However, when they "awake unto God" (see Alma 5:7), amazing changes occur as "the scales of darkness . . . begin to fall from their eyes" (2 Nephi 30:6).

Such was the situation with a young woman who believed that anything was acceptable within their physical relationship now that she and her husband were married. She was highly resistant to the idea that it was possible to be unchaste within marriage until she read the words of President Spencer W. Kimball: "If it is unnatural, you just don't do it. That is all, and all the family life should be kept clean and worthy and on a very high plane. There are some people who have said that behind the bedroom doors anything goes. That is not true and the Lord would not condone it." (*The Teachings of Spencer W. Kimball*, 312.)

These words of a prophet pierced her soul, awakening her. "How could I have been so duped?" she mourned. "Now I can see that I was living in a fog."

As we become increasingly pure, we can see truths we did not see before. And the more open we are to truth, the more pure we become. The more pure we become, the more purified our passions are. And the more pure our passions, the greater our ability to love and to enjoy true marital intimacy. Just think of what awaits those who seek to understand and remember truth!

Chapter 4

LIES THAT
BLIND AND BIND

The story is told of a famous ethologist, Konrad Lorenz, who, in his backyard, experimented with imprinting baby ducklings—that is, getting them to respond to him as if he were their mother. To do so, he walked in a figure eight, crouched over, quacking without interruption while glancing frequently over his shoulders. Dr. Lorenz was congratulating himself on his spectacular feat of getting the baby ducklings to follow him when he looked up—right into the faces of a group of tourists passing by. They were astonished! Lorenz realized that from the tourists' vantage point, the baby ducklings couldn't be seen; they were hidden in the grass. What the onlookers saw was a crazy old man with a long, white beard, making circles and quacking. Without the fuller picture—the ducklings and Lorenz's intent—this brilliant ethologist's imprinting experiment looked like pure craziness! (See Watzlawick, Bavelas, and Jackson, *Pragmatics of Human Communication*, 20.)

An event or concept can never be fully understood until the frame through which we see it is enlarged to include all the elements that are relevant to it. When we seek increased understanding about physical intimacy—which is so sacred, so powerful—we need eternal, wide-angle vision and Spirit-enhanced depth perception!

We live in a fallen world, and the world's approach to love and physical intimacy keeps falling. President Gordon B. Hinckley has said, "Never before, at least not in our generation, have the forces of evil been so blatant, so brazen, so aggressive as they are today." (*Ensign,* November 1998, 98.) The more aberrant the world's approach to intimacy, the more abhorrent it should be to us. However, many succumb to the world's view of intimacy, and their relationships are suffering.

The world is filled with lies about love and sex—lies that then require even more lies to surround them, to shore them up, to make them more believable and palatable, until what has been created is literally a world of lies, a "reality" where nothing is based on eternal truths.

The world's lies are sanctioned as truth because they spew forth from the mouths of articulate, persuasive "experts" and enter our lives through the seemingly "credible" public sources of television, magazines, radio, and the Internet. They are brought to us by the "beautiful people," and sometimes we may think (subconsciously or otherwise) that we want to have lives like theirs. These sophistries can also be brought to us through conversations with our friends and neighbors.

Let's consider just a few of the world's lies about intimacy that hold many individuals and couples captive:

Lie #1: "Love means never having to say 'I'm sorry.'"

Lie #2: "The Church is out of touch with the twenty-first century. The Brethren should update the standards of its moral code. We need to be more loving toward each other these days, and less concerned about people's private sexual behavior."

Lie #3: "Masturbation is normal and healthy."

Lie #4: "I am a victim of my past sexual abuse, my hormones, society, my family, my poor relationships. There is nothing I can do to resist sexual temptations."

Lie #5: "As long as I love my partner, whatever we do is our business. We're not hurting anyone."

Lie #6: "What happens to my body doesn't affect my spirit. They are two very separate entities."

Lie #7: "Sex is dirty and shameful. It's not something that makes you feel joy or love or peace. It's a carnal duty that spouses have to engage in from time to time in order to have children."

Lie #8: "We had a temple wedding; therefore we have a temple marriage. We were sealed, so it really doesn't matter how we treat each other now or how moral our behavior is. We're together forever."

Lie #9: "If I have a sexual urge, I need to act on it. To try to suppress those feelings would be unnatural and unhealthy."

Lie #10: "If my spouse says 'No' to any of my sexual advances or suggestions, it means he or she doesn't really love me."

Lie #11: "I always feel loved when I'm with my colleague. He's my best friend, and he really loves me and takes care of me. An affair of the heart can't hurt anything."

Lie #12: "If you are having sexual problems the best thing you can do is to rent some X-rated movies, read a romance novel, or buy a skimpy negligee."

And now for one truth: "Thus the devil cheateth their souls, and leadeth them away carefully down to hell." (2 Nephi 28:21.)

LUCIFER'S LIES

Lucifer is like an evil eye surgeon who blinds us, a cruel cardiologist who hardens our hearts, a grand distortionist who makes crooked things look straight and straight things look crooked.

One distressed husband was ready to give up on his marriage. After all he had done to try to help his marriage, why should he keep trying? He couldn't believe how unreasonable his wife was. She was cold and frigid, and he was sick and tired of feeling like a pervert just because he wanted to have sex with his wife!

What had happened? He had invited his wife to attend an exciting basketball game out of town. He wanted to "add some spice" to their physical relationship, which had been almost nil and highly unsatisfying to them both. His solution? He asked her to remove her temple garments before traveling out of town for the evening and gave her exotic, erotic undergarments to wear instead.

He imagined it would all be so thrilling. They would be the only ones who would know "their secret," and he believed that her passion would escalate along with his throughout the evening, bringing them both to a fever pitch that they would satisfy at a cozy hotel immediately following the basketball game. His hopes were dashed when she said adamantly and with horror, "No! I won't remove my garments! You're asking me to break my temple covenants!"

What was she talking about? She wouldn't remove her garments? Why not? She must be crazy! She'd taken this "spiritual" thing way too far.

Each spouse was in distress. She was horrified by his request; he was stunned by her horror. His idea seemed so logical and even loving to him! He couldn't see that he had fallen for Lucifer's lustful substitute for true intimacy.

Lucifer is the father of all lies, the master of deceit and illusion, the creator of chaos and confusion. He can make wrong look and feel right, and right feel unloving and naive.

The truth about Satan is that he hates truth! He loves lies and will hand you a lie tailor-made to your vulnerabilities, any day, any time you open yourself up to him. His greatest desire is that the lie—which will now look like the truth—will entice you, even slightly, to turn from the truth and turn your life over to him. And his greatest triumph comes when you believe that your sins are not sins at all.

Satan's vision of physical intimacy is cunning, counterfeiting, contorting, and as old as time itself. If you wonder how really old the adversary's craftiness is, and therefore how really good he is at his craft, just read Romans 1:24–31 and 2 Timothy 3:1–6. There, in black and white, is a description of what we can see in living color in our own homes, with the assistance of our televisions, VCRs, and computers. Paul's account of the sins of the people—who once knew God and yet turned away—sounds just like one night's worth of prime-time sitcoms.

Here is Paul's report:

"[They were] filled with all unrighteousness, fornication, wickedness, covetousness, maliciousness, full of envy, murder, debate, deceit, malignity. . . . [They were] backbiters, haters of God, despiteful, proud, boasters, inventors of evil things, disobedient to parents, without understanding, covenantbreakers, without natural affection, implacable, unmerciful." (Romans 1:29–31.)

Now, listen as Paul describes for Timothy the last days—our days! As you listen, think about where you may have seen these things before:

"In the last days perilous times shall come. For men shall be lovers of their own selves, covetous, boasters, proud, blasphemers, disobedient to parents, unthankful, unholy, without natural affection, trucebreakers, false accusers, incontinent, fierce, despisers of those that are good, traitors, heady, highminded, lovers of pleasures more than lovers of God." (2 Timothy 3:1–4.) We've lived to see this in the world around us.

And then the most chilling message of all: It's not bad enough that those horrible things are happening out there in the world. The worst part is that they come sneaking and creeping into our homes to influence us! Listen to verse 6: "Of this sort are they which creep into houses, and lead captive silly women laden with sins, led away with divers lusts." (2 Timothy 3:6.)

Could Paul possibly be talking about afternoon soap operas and late-night talk shows? And could he be describing those of us who watch them? Are we silly when we watch them? Is watching them leading us away into divers lusts?

Could Isaiah possibly be speaking to us, the Lord's men and women of the latter days, when he says, "Rise up, ye women [and men] that are at ease; hear my voice, ye careless daughters [and sons]." (Isaiah 32:9.)

Regrettably, many of us have been too careless. We have drifted in the direction of the world's view. Our only recourse is to "rise up"—and to be careful! We need to be vigilant about anything that comes into our hearts, minds, and homes pertaining to physical intimacy. We must be careful with our language and our conversations about everything related to this sacred physical gift.

Think about all those whose lives, in one way or another, have been shattered and shackled because of the effects of moral transgressions. To protect our minds and hearts, our homes and families from the intrusions of the devil's devices, perhaps we need big, bold warning signs on every book, magazine, videotape, audiotape, sitcom, movie, and play co-produced by the adversary himself. Such signs would reveal his works for what they are: his angry protests against God and his persistent, power-hungry efforts to obliterate the truth!

Warning #1—to be stamped on the covers of his magazines: "Contents highly addictive. Extremely corrosive-to-the-soul materials enclosed. Be prepared to have your mind twisted, your views of love ravaged, and your spirit shrunk. Be aware that the Spirit of the Lord will not be with you during or after viewing. Be prepared that after an initial rush, you will experience feelings of depression, loneliness, despair, and guilt. However, with repeated exposures over time, you can numb those feelings—and enter into almost total amnesia about who you really are and about the truth itself."

Warning #2—for the beginning of Satan's co-produced movies: "The following scenes are brought to you in the hopes that you will think of yourself as an animal. Actually, the dung from an animal is more pure and would harm you less if taken into your system! Extreme caution needed. This movie will make you believe that lust is really love—and that all love really is, is lust!

This movie will have its greatest effect if watched when you feel misunderstood, alone, blue, or simply that you don't fit in. If you aren't in any of those moods, watching the movie will actually help you get there.

Warning #3—for the devil's Internet sites: "Share the following with someone whose soul you would like to destroy. Complete success is ensured if you can offer it in the spirit of friendship and under the guise of love. By thinking and talking together about the content, all sweet, pure feelings will be distorted into grand perversions. Pick a perversion—any perversion. That, in fact, may be one of the last choices you will get to make. In fact, if you're tired of making choices, just view the following several times—or keep immersing yourself in similar material—and your freedom will be increasingly limited with each viewing. The irony is that you will have the illusion that your freedom is actually increasing! We've taken this way beyond the old smoke-and-mirrors tricks, and the illusions that will deceive your heart and mind will be stunning! Virtual reality is here to replace virtuous living."

Warning #4—to announce the adversary's influence on prime-time viewing: "How many lies can you find in the following sitcom? If you can't find any—gotcha! In the following, we'll offer you ideas that you've never before entertained! But, with repetition and humor, we'll slowly dilute the initial recoiling of your spirit—and you'll begin to forget that there was ever a time when you didn't believe these lies to be true."

Warning #5—for rental videos that support the adversary's agenda: "Fantasy only allowed here. Only erotic illusions are included. No empathetic love is depicted. No consequences are noted. No impact on your body, your spirit, or your relationships with God, family, and friends will be addressed. Please note that interactions will appear much more splendid than they really are. This is not real life! But it is a really great lie! We've left out the dire consequences that would only ruin the subtle appeal this movie will have for you."

Warning #6—for purchased videos that support the adversary's agenda: "Congratulations! You bought the movie this time instead of just renting it! Actually, you're buying this whole scheme: hook, line, and sinker. Let's just have this be our little secret. No one needs to know. No one will ever notice. When people tell you that you look different or talk differently or are more difficult to get along with, just get angry at them and go buy another movie or magazine with similar contents. Actually, you'll soon be ready to advance to our total-destruction-of-the-senses line. You, too, will soon be past feeling!"

And if those six warnings aren't heeded? That brings us to an intermission announcement, which is: "We'll soon be taking a commercial break. You, on the other hand, who are now a bit more dull in your thinking—a little more under the spell of adversary-induced amnesia—you are now primed for a different kind of break. How about breaking your covenants? Breaking your spouse's heart? Breaking apart your marriage? Breaking your children's and parents' and siblings' and friends' hearts? All of these breaks that you never thought possible are now just a little more within your reach."

One active Latter-day Saint woman acknowledged that it was after watching a certain popular movie that she first started thinking about having an affair with the man who was building her family's new home. She had the affair. Her house was built. Her marriage was destroyed. Those involved now live in three separate houses: the builder (it seems strange to call him that) with his wife in their original house; the woman with some of her children in another; and the ex-husband and the rest of the children in yet another. No one lives in the house that was built while this woman's home was being destroyed.

It's time to make certain that Satan does not have a grip on our hearts, minds, homes, and families. If we find any evidence of his blatantly obvious or even his covertly subtle presence, we need to cast him out! We need to do more than just loosen his grip; we need to completely get rid of him so that we can be taught by the Spirit truths about intimacy that will strengthen our marriages.

As you and your spouse prayerfully seek the Lord's guidance, you will come to know what you can do right now to determine if the adversary's impure influence is in your life—and how to remove it. It may be time for some serious spring cleaning!

Chapter 5

THE ALIENATING
INFLUENCE OF ANGER

We have spoken of impurity and worldly views of love and sex as obstacles to marital intimacy. Now let's consider another influence that can creep into a relationship and wreak havoc: anger.

Anger kills love and alienates intimacy. As Mormon mourned to his son Moroni about the state of the Nephites: "So exceedingly do they anger that it seemeth me that they have no fear of death; and they have lost their love, one towards another." (Moroni 9:5.)

For spouses who are serious about marital intimacy, it's time to kick anger out of their lives—or, stated a little less violently, it's time to put anger away. Contentions are not of God. (See 3 Nephi 11:29–30.) As men and women of God we need to heed Paul's counsel: "Put off all these; anger, wrath, malice, blasphemy, filthy communication out of your mouth." (Colossians 3:8.) Spouses cannot expect to have access to the power, delight, love, light, and peace of true marital intimacy if anger is present. Emotional violence, the antithesis of love, takes over. Anger and emotional violence are a demoralizing duo.

What Is Emotional Violence?

Emotional violence has been defined as "holding an idea to be true, such that another's idea is wrong and must change." (H. R. Maturana, "Biology, Emotions and Culture.") It is the *and must change* aspect that brings about emotional violence. Thus, anger and emotional violence arise when one spouse believes that he or she is more correct than the other—and that the other's ideas *must* change.

For spouses to be passionate about their ideas is one thing— perhaps even a great thing. Offering ideas to one another and understanding that each spouse holds different ideas can be the essence of a congenial discussion—even merging into a warm disputation. A wife offers her idea; her husband offers his. No problems arise. But when one spouse says—either directly or indirectly—"You *must* change your view," emotional violence enters in. Requiring that your spouse must change his or her thoughts, feelings, or behavior is more than demanding—it is demonic!

President Howard W. Hunter pointed out the Lord's approach to influencing others: "God's chief way of acting is by persuasion and patience and long-suffering, not by coercion and stark confrontation. He acts by gentle solicitation and by sweet enticement. He always acts with unfailing respect for the freedom and independence that we possess." (*Ensign,* November 1989, 18.)

One of our hymns, "Know This, That Every Soul Is Free," expresses these same truths:

> He'll call, persuade, direct aright,
> And bless with wisdom, love, and light,
> In nameless ways be good and kind,
> But never force the human mind.
>
> (*Hymns,* no. 240.)

Spouses cannot *make* each other change their minds. But they can invite and entice, offer and persuade—and then respect what the other chooses to do.

Have anger and emotional violence crept into your relationship, killing—or at least wounding—your marital intimacy? Do you always *have* to be right? What could you do to diminish, even just a little, the hold that anger and emotional violence may have on your life?

A CLOWN OR A CIRCUS?

Multiple perspectives can be represented by a picture that looks like a clown—until it is turned sideways. Then it looks like a whole circus. Metaphorically, spouses in conflict perpetually debate the "truth" of what is in the picture. The husband says (so to speak), "This is a picture of a clown." And the wife says, "You've got to be kidding. This is a picture of a whole circus!" Viewing the clown-circus picture from different points of view, each sees something different.

The two different perspectives can be intriguing and could actually be used to build the relationship if spouses remained kind and curious: "Help me understand how you are able to see the clown." "Show me where you see the circus." However, when one spouse, or both, holds the belief, "There is one correct view and I have it—and you must have it too!" then emotional violence begins. Negative characterizations, recriminations, and accusations flow, either stated or implied: "You are so stupid if you can't see that this is a circus." "If you had half a brain you'd see the clown!" "I'd be able to see the circus if you weren't in my way." And thus the caustic wounding of souls continues.

Cruel words hit and bruise just as forcefully as a physical slap, punch, or slug. And they diminish and prevent true marital intimacy.

One wife spoke about the cruel words of her husband, noting that the pain she felt from his words was the worst she had ever felt. "I think the word *stupid* is the meanest word in the whole world," she said, "because I've heard it so much. I'm not stupid. I know I'm not. But still it hurts to hear it coming from the person I love. When he says that, it makes me feel so bad. My soul wants to run away and hide. But I can't hide because this is my marriage."

Another woman spoke in defense of her own attacking words toward her husband: "Well, I'm just trying to 'reprove with sharpness.' Isn't that what the Lord tells us to do?" As Elder H. Burke Peterson pointed out, "Reproving with sharpness means reproving with clarity, with loving firmness, with serious intent. It does not mean reproving with sarcasm, or with bitterness, or with clenched teeth and raised voice. One who reproves as the Lord has directed deals in principles, not personalities. He does not attack character or demean an individual." (*Ensign*, July 1989, 10.)

CO-CREATING ANGER

Most often anger is co-created—that is, both spouses have a role in its escalation. Consider one couple's experience. The wife described the development of her anger: "He never helps with the children. And then he wants to be physically affectionate at the kitchen sink. Give me a break! How many different ways can I say 'Leave me alone, I have other things to do'?"

Her husband described the development of his anger: "I give up. I've done everything I can do, and it's never enough and it's never right. I'm criticized about seven times an hour. If I read my scriptures, I should be helping with the dishes. If I'm working on my computer, I should be reading my scriptures. It turns me right off the scriptures because she controls everything about them. There is apparently a time and a place for everything. But I'm never going to be able to figure out the time or the place for anything."

Spouses too often spend their time trying to convince each

other of the error of each other's views. Emotional violence increases and the spouses indeed "[lose] their love, one towards another." (Moroni 9:5.)

WHAT ABOUT "WARRANTED" ANGER?

Is it ever right for a wife to verbally hit her husband with words like these: "You are so selfish and stupid you deserve to go to hell"? (Criticism.) Is it ever okay for a husband to throw the scriptures at his wife, or to pull all the covers off the bed, wrapping them around himself as he kneels at the opposite side of the bed from his wife, refusing to pray? (Rejection.) Is it ever correct for a wife to persistently be late for business dinners her husband is hosting? (Undermining.) Is it ever acceptable for a husband to consistently turn a deaf ear to his wife's requests for time together? (Negation.)

According to the Lord's words, it is not, for "whosoever is angry with his brother without a cause shall be in danger of the judgment." (Matthew 5:22.) That sounds severe enough, but at least there is that marvelous loophole of "without a cause." It seems as though we can almost always figure out "a cause." But in 3 Nephi 12:22 the words "without a cause" are removed. What a crushing blow against coming to blows!

But what if there really are legitimate concerns and frustrations? Does the Lord really mean "*whosoever* is angry with his brother shall be in danger of his judgment"—meaning anyone, anytime? Does the Lord really intend that spouses should *never* be angry with each other? Even if your wife has criticized you for everything from your parenting skills to the number of cookies you just ate, and you can't stand it another minute? Even if your husband refuses to do the small and simple things you ask him to do? "How can I not get angry if these things keep happening?" you may protest.

Note the importance of understanding the perspective of both husband and wife. The husband experiences his wife as always criticizing him, but what would the wife's description be? The wife experiences her husband as negating her, but how does the husband see the situation? Each spouse will have his or her version of the "truth," of what is really happening.

Once again, anger is generated when at least one spouse believes that his or her view is the most correct one. And anger builds as he or she holds tightly to the "correct view," insisting that the other spouse's view *must* change.

A TRIO OF TROUBLE

Spouses who believe that they are the most correct tend to do at least three other things when responding to a situation:

1. They rush to judgment.

2. They accuse their spouses of negative intent—that is, of being intentionally cruel, mean, hurtful, or unloving.

3. They fail to remember that things are often not as they appear to be.

The situation between Captain Moroni and Pahoran is a great example of this trio of trouble. In Alma 59, Moroni writes his first letter to Pahoran requesting assistance to strengthen the forces of Helaman. As conditions worsen, so does Moroni's outlook.

In his next letter (Alma 60), Moroni accuses Pahoran of everything from selfishness and neglect to malevolent intent. His accusations include: "Can you think to sit upon your thrones in a state of thoughtless stupor?" and "Ye have withheld your provisions."

Pahoran's response to Captain Moroni helps us understand how we can escape from the trio of trouble, how a spouse can avoid being angry when negative things are happening. Rather than lashing back with something like, "How can you expect me to help you with an attitude like that!" Pahoran says: "In your epistle you have censured me, but it mattereth not; I am not angry, but do rejoice in the greatness of your heart." (Alma 61:9.)

How does Pahoran manage such a response? Pahoran looks through all of Moroni's overtly negative behavior and sees "the greatness of [Moroni's] heart"—and rejoices! He seems to have attributed benevolent intent to Moroni's malevolent words, assuming that Moroni was up to something good, even in the midst of his censuring. Pahoran's response to Captain Moroni's outburst is a marvelous guide for responding to false accusations, negative characterizations, and recriminations.

When a husband falsely accuses his wife of betraying him to his family, or when a wife negatively characterizes her husband as lazy and unhelpful, is it still possible for the accused to see the accuser's good heart, even the accuser's great heart? When husbands and wives follow Pahoran's example, it is. Pahoran's kind of response heals relationships because it invites the Spirit to be present.

An important aside: One caution is obvious. Seeing an accuser's great heart (that is, trying to understand that person's needs or motives) is very different from assuming that a chronic abuser is going to change—without something else changing. In the latter case, taking action to leave the situation is usually best for all involved.

COULD IT BE UNRIGHTEOUS DOMINION?

One wife realized that her desire to control—even "micromanage"—everything was inviting anger into their marriage. Her husband realized that the frustration that fed his aggression grew from his belief that he couldn't influence anything, including his wife's opinion of him. After reviewing Elder H. Burke Peterson's questions identifying unrighteous dominion (*Ensign,* July 1989, 10), each spouse recognized that unrighteous dominion was a problem for both of them.

Consider the following questions, which have been adapted from Elder Peterson's. Which of these questions for detecting unrighteous dominion might help you look closer at yourself, your spouse, and your marriage?

1. As one who believes in the doctrine of agency, how do I guard and protect the agency of my spouse?

2. Do I ever behave in ways my spouse experiences as intimidating? As taking away my spouse's choices? As discounting my spouse's thoughts and feelings?

3. Do I criticize more than I compliment my spouse?

4. Do I insist that my spouse obey me and do everything my way?

5. Do I attempt to guarantee my place of authority with my spouse by physical means (discipline or punishment)?

6. Do I find myself setting and enforcing rules to control my spouse?

7. How do I invite my spouse to come closer to the Savior?

8. Do I see my spouse as my sister or brother who needs my help to return to Heavenly Father? How does viewing my spouse in this way influence my behavior in our marriage—in both good ways and bad?

9. Does my spouse appear to be fearful of me?

10. Do I feel threatened by the prospect of sharing with my spouse the power and responsibility for decision making in matters that affect each of us?

11. Does my spouse seem reluctant to talk to me about some of his or her feelings and concerns?

12. Do I appear to my spouse that I can never be wrong—by what I say, how I look, how I sound, or my unwillingness to ask for and appreciate his or her feedback?

13. What beliefs about "being right" or "winning and losing" do I have that keep my spouse from making decisions, expressing feelings and thoughts, or feeling safe when we're together?

14. Do I do things that make my spouse highly dependent on me so that my spouse has difficulty making his or her own decisions?

15. Do I withhold money, love, or affection as a way of controlling my spouse and influencing our relationship?

16. Do I insist on being the main source of inspiration rather than expecting my spouse to listen to the Spirit?

17. Do I often feel angry and critical toward my spouse because I think he or she isn't doing things the way I think they should be done?

18. How does my spouse experience my best intentions to live the gospel fully? As oppressive or loving? As constraining or freeing?

19. What would I look for in my spouse that would tell me that, despite the sincere intentions of my heart, he or she sees me as exercising unrighteous dominion?

20. If I see my spouse as exercising unrighteous dominion, how can I respond so I don't escalate the problem? (From Harper and Watson, unpublished questionnaire.)

Unrighteous dominion has many faces. Two are anger and emotional violence. Anger and emotional violence harden hearts, blind eyes, deafen ears, and darken minds. Marital intimacy is dramatically diminished, if not annihilated, when the anger and emotional violence of unrighteous dominion are present. Why? Because unrighteous dominion oppresses and negates your spouse. No relationship is possible because your spouse has been obliterated. All that is left is you—you, "married" to your "correct" view of life, lonely and unfulfilled. And thus the high consequences of unrighteous dominion escalate.

Fortunately, however, as we will see in the following chapter, change is always possible.

PART 3

INCREASING INTIMACY IN YOUR MARRIAGE

Marriage can be more an exultant ecstasy
than the human mind can conceive.
—Spencer W. Kimball,
BYU Speeches of the Year,
1976, 146

Chapter 6

CHANGE IS
ALWAYS POSSIBLE

Can we really change? Of course we can! Even with all the lies about love, all the false traditions of the world, all the personal obstacles—constraining thoughts, constricting feelings, consuming and conflicting behaviors—is it *really* possible for a couple to change their pattern of interaction so they can experience marital intimacy in a way they never have before? The answer is yes. But how? Paul said it best: "Let us lay aside every weight, and the sin which doth so easily beset us and let us run with patience the race that is set before us." (Hebrews 12:1.)

We can lay aside the anger, the selfishness, the pride, the fear, the misconceptions and lies, and the personal impurity that may afflict us. Spouses can't run the race that is set before them while carrying such heavy burdens. And marital intimacy is always elusive for spouses whose energies are being spent carrying excess baggage.

How different would your marriage be if you could lay aside

the things that weigh you and your spouse down? What weight is impeding your "race"? Is it anger that trips you up from time to time? Is it fear that sneaks into your life uninvited? Is pornography pulling you off course? Are overcommitment and stress getting in your way? Are critical words from the past still haunting you?

One woman overheard her father giving last-minute coaching instructions to her husband the day before they were married: "She'll always need someone to take care of her." Those words invited oppression and depression into their lives for thirty years. Her husband believed that he had been given a sanction to "be the boss"—her boss. And she believed that she was not capable of influencing her own life.

What change would make the biggest difference to your marital intimacy? Would it be a change in the way you see yourself, or in the way you believe your spouse sees you? Would it be a change in your spouse's beliefs about marital intimacy? A change in your ability to give up your favorite sins? A change in the weight of the burdens on your spouse's mind? Or do you most desire a change in your nature, a change of heart?

Let's talk about six ways to invite change into your life—six ways to increase the possibility of change in your marital intimacy.

BELIEFS OF THE HEART

1. Change is possible when the belief at the heart of the matter is discovered.

Ancient Hebrew tradition held that the heart could think. If we are to invite change into our lives, we need to uncover our heart-generated and heartfelt thoughts, those saturated with feelings. These are the beliefs of the heart that influence all we do, think, and feel. These are the beliefs that provide the greatest leverage for change, core beliefs that can either constrain or facilitate change. Constraining beliefs decrease the possibility of change. Facilitating beliefs increase the possibility of change. (See

Wright, Watson, and Bell, *Beliefs: The Heart of Healing in Families and Illness*.)

One couple, hurting from years of building walls to protect their hearts, wondered why they felt so lonely. The core belief that held each of them captive, preventing them from reaching out to each other at the very time they needed each other the most, was, "I am not lovable and not worthy of love."

A woman, ruled by anger that oppressed her husband, her children, and herself, held to the belief, "There is one correct view, and I have it." This constraining belief invited frustration, anger, and unrighteous dominion into her marital relationship.

A couple struggling to find new ways of relating with each other after twenty-five years of silence and suffering believed, "My spouse doesn't care about my feelings and what life in our marriage has been like for me." Each spouse felt misunderstood and underappreciated.

A young husband seeking assistance in his almost lifelong battle with pornography believed, "I am weak!" This belief discouraged him and invited him to withdraw from his wife in every way: physically, emotionally, spiritually, mentally, and socially, and thus to be even more vulnerable to pornography's pull.

All of these spouses' heart-held beliefs prevented them from finding solutions and instead invited the most constraining belief of all—that a solution was impossible! However, once the constraining beliefs were identified, they could be replaced by facilitating beliefs such as: "My spouse loved me enough to make a sacred covenant to spend eternity with me. We can build on that love." "There are many different ways to look at things." "My spouse cares about my feelings and has been showing me, in ways different from expected, how much I am appreciated." "With the Savior's help and my spouse's help, I am strong."

What old, constraining beliefs might be preventing you and your spouse from experiencing true marital intimacy? What new, facilitating belief would move you and your spouse even one step closer to passion that is purified and therefore magnified? What would need to happen for you to embrace this new, facilitating belief so that you could embrace your spouse in a whole new way?

REFLECTION

2. Change is possible through the process of reflection.

"The moment of reflection . . . is the moment when we become aware of that part of ourselves which we cannot see in any other way." (Maturana and Varela, *The Tree of Knowledge.*) We experience the process of reflection when we look into a mirror; there we see an image we would not otherwise be able to see. The same thing can happen spiritually and emotionally, as through reflection we become aware of ourselves, others, and situations in a whole new way. Consider President Joseph F. Smith's experience as recorded in Doctrine and Covenants 138. In a state of "pondering" and "reflecting," he came to a new understanding of life after death.

The possibility for change is increased when we are invited to reflect. "I never knew . . ." is a frequent response following a reflection. Reflecting about our situation helps us see and think about it differently. Then we start feeling differently and behaving differently. Thus reflection increases the possibility of change.

Alma the Younger was passionate about change and an expert at asking questions that invited others to reflect so that change in their lives might occur. In Alma 5 alone there are more than forty such questions, including: "Have ye received his image in your countenances?" "Have ye experienced this mighty change in your hearts?" "If ye have experienced a change of heart, and if ye have felt to sing the song of redeeming love, . . . can ye feel so now?" (Alma 5:14, 26.)

Through his persistent questioning, Alma invites us to reflect over and over on our status with the Lord, on our present spiritual development, on things we need to change or have changed—and before we know it, our desire for more change increases.

The next time you want an incredible experience with reflection—to see what it feels like to be invited and enticed to change—read and ponder Alma 5, maybe several times. Notice how your thoughts about yourself, your spouse, and your possibilities for change are altered through Alma's persistent questioning.

Perhaps you and your spouse have reflected lately on certain questions that keep coming to your minds. How do the questions that you ask yourself on a good day compare with those on a bad day? Many spouses seeking true marital intimacy ask themselves such questions as "Am I worthy *of* love?" "Am I worthy *to* love?" "Have I been forgiven of my sins?" "Am I clean before the Lord?" "What else can I do to strengthen our marriage?" and "How does my spouse experience my love for him or her inside *and* outside our bedroom?"

Asking questions is just one way to invite reflection and increase the likelihood of change. Unexpected events—from a natural disaster to the seemingly premature death of a loved one—also invite reflection. Anything that catches and focuses our attention can help us think about things we hadn't considered before, and to see things in a whole new way.

One husband reflected on his marriage and his life when his wife was finally able to articulate that she believed that he did not see her as his equal and that nothing she had contributed to their marriage had made a difference to him.

His response was deep grief, which was born of a new understanding. "I never knew," he said, "that I had caused her this much pain." He had not realized the influence his past unkind and thoughtless words had had on his wife's heart and mind. With this new understanding, he determined to change how he talked with and treated her.

Voices of Authority

3. Change is possible when voices of authority speak healing words.

In the previous example, the husband's voice was a "voice of authority" for his wife. This means simply that what he said mattered to her and influenced her view of herself. Who is *your* voice of authority? Which voices constrain change in your life? Which voices support and sustain the changes you so desire?

Change is possible when voices of authority speak healing and encouraging words. Words like: "You can do it," or "I knew you had it in you." Words of apology and forgiveness. Change is promoted when voices of authority inspire you to be who you really are, to speak up about what's really in your heart, and to listen to the voice of the Lord in your life.

When couples are seeking to change, they need to be aware of chiding voices, mocking voices, strident voices that may have slipped into their lives, minds, and hearts, silencing their own inner voice. Some voices cleverly call "obedience" a far too simple-minded approach to life. Others are so sophisticated in their disparagement of truth that couples start to believe they are missing something in their own assessments.

Here are some questions for you to consider regarding the voices you choose to listen to and project:

• Is your spouse's voice a voice of authority in your life? If so, what words are you longing to hear?

• If your spouse's voice is not a voice of authority in your life, what would need to change in order for it to become so?

• Are you a voice of authority in your spouse's life? (Remember, if you are, it matters to your spouse what you think about him or her—and how you express those feelings and thoughts.)

• Are you the keeper of some words that would make all the difference in your spouse's life?

- Are you willing to speak words of healing, comfort, and cheer to your spouse?
- Have you already received clues about what your spouse is longing to hear from you?
- What would need to be different for you to be able to offer those words honestly from your heart?
- Have you unwittingly been silencing your spouse's voice—through your sermonettes, through your overexplanations and defenses of your actions, or through asking, "Why did you do that?" and yet never accepting his or her explanations or apologies?

Change is also possible when the ears of those who are voices of authority take time and care to listen. As the voice of authority in your spouse's life, you need to listen—and to ask: "Tell me about the pain you felt because of what I did—or someone else did. Tell me. Tell me more." Ask and listen: "Tell me about the joy you feel now because of the decision you made. Tell me. Tell me more." An extra level of healing occurs when your ears of authority are open to hear the exquisiteness of your spouse's pain and joy. Change is accelerated!

And yet, as helpful as human voices of authority are, none can or should replace the ultimate voice of authority, the Word Himself, the Savior Jesus Christ. What are you and your spouse doing to hear His voice in your lives? What are you doing to establish His voice as the voice of authority for you and your marriage? The voice of the Lord will strengthen your voice and provide direction and courage—especially for those times when you need to speak the unspeakable. And for some spouses, "the unspeakable" that they most need to say to each other is "I really do love you." "I really need you in my life." "I am so sorry!" "I forgive you."

Who You Really Are

4. *Change is possible when spouses are true to who they really are.*

As you learn to hear the voice of the Lord in your life, you and your spouse will increasingly be able to hear who you really are. A story is told of a caterpillar named Yellow who was trying to discover what she should do with her life. In her wanderings she came upon another caterpillar caught in some gauzy filament. Concerned, she asked if she could help. The other caterpillar explained that the filament was all part of becoming a butterfly. When Yellow heard the word *butterfly*, her whole insides leaped. "But what is a butterfly?" she asked. The cocooned caterpillar explained, "It's what you are meant to become." Yellow was intrigued but a bit defiant: "How can I believe there's a butterfly inside you or me when all I see is a fuzzy worm?" After further reflection she pensively asked, "How does one become a butterfly?" And the answer? "You must want to fly so much that you are willing to give up being a caterpillar." (Trina Paulus, *Hope for the Flowers.*)

What are you willing to give up being so that you can fly? Your spirit wants to fly. Influenced by the Spirit, your spirit can stir with fleeting memories of your premortal accomplishments and commitments. Is that too difficult to believe?

Perhaps the words of Lorenzo Snow will help: "Jesus was a god before he came into the world and yet his knowledge was taken from him. He did not know his former greatness, neither do we know what greatness we had attained to before we came here." (*Official Journal of Lorenzo Snow*, 8 October 1900, 181–82.)

Are there marvelous words, recurring phrases, lofty thoughts, grand concepts, memorable people, unforgettable places, compelling scriptures, and haunting music that make your heart and spirit leap up? Perhaps these internal leapings are premortal stirrings—brief glimpses of your premortal life. They just may be brief tutorings about who you really are—and as Sheri L. Dew has taught, "who you have always been." (BYU Women's Conference 2001.)

Consider the fact that you were valiant before you came to earth, that you have to pass through an ordeal here without remembering what you were like premortally or knowing the importance of your mission here on earth. What would you be willing to give up being—thinking, feeling, doing, and saying—in order to be all that you really are?

Change is possible as spouses honor their premortal stirrings and rise up as the men and women of God they really are. Perhaps now is the perfect time to give up living beneath yourself, to give up the thoughts, feelings, and actions that keep you and your spouse groveling on the ground when you could be flying, even soaring! Perhaps now is the time to lift your sights and to cocoon yourself away from the old caterpillar way of life so that your real self can emerge.

What would such "cocooning" be for you? Think of Alma and his life-changing cocooning process. His cocooning included harrowing-up reflections about his past as well as comforting memories of his father's teachings about the Atonement. From the depths of his soul Alma cried out, "O Jesus, thou Son of God, have mercy on me, who am in the gall of bitterness, and am encircled about by the everlasting chains of death." (Alma 36:18.) Many spouses understand the anguish that prompted Alma's pleading. And, happily, many are no longer strangers to the joy Alma experienced and expressed: "Oh, what joy, and what marvelous light I did behold; yea my soul was filled with joy as exceeding as was my pain!" (Alma 36:20.)

LOVE

5. Change is possible when love is present.

Love is the greatest invitation for change. The Prophet Joseph Smith said of the power of love, "Nothing is so much calculated to lead people to forsake sin as to take them by the hand, and watch over them with tenderness. When persons manifest the least kindness and love to me, O what power it has over my mind, while the opposite course has a tendency to harrow up all the harsh feelings and depress the human mind." (*Teachings of the Prophet Joseph Smith,* 240.)

The presence of true love that both husband and wife can feel and within which they both feel secure is indeed the greatest motivator for change.

THE SAVIOR: THE ULTIMATE SOURCE FOR CHANGE

6. Change always occurs as we come closer to the Savior and become more like Him.

The Savior entreats us to come unto Him. He wants us to come close to Him. He wants us to get to know Him and not just know about Him. As we come closer to the Savior, we can become more like Him. How can this happen? Perhaps a principle from biology can help us understand.

The biological principle of "structural coupling" proffers that the more we repeatedly interact with someone or something over time, the more we become like that person or thing. (See Maturana and Varela, *The Tree of Knowledge.*) Thus, as we interact more and more with the Savior, as we "structurally couple" with Him, we can become increasingly like Him. And since He never changes (see 3 Nephi 24:6), all the changes that occur as we interact with Him will be in us.

Paul explains that the key to laying aside "every weight, and the sin which doth so easily beset us" and to running "with patience the race that is set before us" is to look to the Savior as "the author and finisher of our faith." (Hebrews 12:1–2.) Spouses who look to the Savior for the power to change will run with patience the race that is set before them and embrace eternal truths about marital intimacy that will dramatically change their lives.

The Savior is the ultimate source of all change. He changed water into wine, bringing the very best liquid refreshment to the celebration—and He will bring the very best out in you and your spouse as you turn to Him. He will rescue all that is finest inside you. Ask. Asking for the Savior's help will bring you and your spouse closer to Him.

The Savior changed eyes—and He can give you and your spouse the eyes to see what you need to see in order to increase your marital intimacy. He will open the eyes of your understanding.

The Savior changed ears—and He can help you hear what your spouse is really trying to say.

The Savior changed limbs that were weak—and He can give you and your spouse the ability to move toward true marital intimacy.

The Savior changed a few fishes and loaves of bread into enough food to feed five thousand people—and He will magnify your widow's mites of time, energy, and capacities so there is enough and to spare.

He changed names—Saul became Paul, and He can help you and your spouse become His son and daughter and thus take upon you His name in a whole new way.

And although He Himself never changes, He is the quintessential change agent—the only true change agent. What a splendid irony! There is only one true and living change agent—and He changes not. He loves you and your spouse and your efforts to change. His desire is for you both to change, to have a change of heart, a change of nature, and thus, over time, to completely cast off the natural man and the natural woman.

The Savior did all that He did so that we could change. He is our Savior! As we actively and persistently plead for the power of His infinite and atoning sacrifice to be applied to our lives, His ultimate healing will bring to us the ultimate change we need.

CONCLUSION

As we look to the Savior for wisdom and courage to do the seemingly impossible, giving Him every weight and sin of ours, He will lighten our burdens so we will not feel them upon our backs. (See Mosiah 24:14.) He will help us change. And as we look *to* Him, we can come to look *like* Him—having His image engraven upon our countenances—and to look at the world and each other as He does.

Unlike anger, fear, pain, lies, and misconceptions that seem to barge into our lives, the Savior will not force His way in. He will not use the megaphone of man and stand outside homes and hearts shouting, "Put your burdens down. Move away from your burdens." But He will stand outside and knock. And He will send His messenger, the Holy Ghost, to whisper truth.

Among the truths the Spirit will bear witness to you, as you seek to hear, is that change is always possible.

Change is possible when the belief at the heart of the matter is discovered.

It is possible through the process of reflection.

It is possible when voices of authority speak healing words.

It is possible when spouses are true to who they really are.

It is possible when love is present.

And change always occurs as we come closer to the Savior and become more like Him.

Chapter 7

THE HEALING POWER OF APOLOGIES AND FORGIVENESS

Y ou and your spouse are the keepers of two seemingly simple phrases that can make all the difference to your marital intimacy when you exchange them with sincere intent. "I am sorry" is a phrase that is packed with power, especially when it is responded to with a similarly potent phrase: "I forgive you."

If you and your spouse can both offer and accept apologies, you can solve literally any problem and you can dramatically increase your ability to experience the truths and joys of marital intimacy. Apologies and forgiveness clear away debris that otherwise prevents the union of spouses' bodies and spirits, the union of their lives, and their unity with the Lord. It's amazing to think that six words, "I am sorry" and "I forgive you," can do so much to enhance the meaning of "I love you," but they can.

President Gordon B. Hinckley has pleaded with men who

have been verbally or emotionally abusive toward their wives and children to apologize to them. (See *Ensign*, November 1996, 68.) Surely, he would offer the same counsel to women. However, some spouses find it extremely difficult to apologize for their wrongdoings. One wife did what all too many do: She apologized to her family for her angry, emotionally violent outbursts and then reneged, saying she should never have had to apologize in the first place. She found the whole thing "too demeaning" and was certain it made her look bad. She stated adamantly that if her family really understood the Atonement, they would forgive her without her needing to apologize! This woman didn't understand her own responsibility in accessing the healing power that is in the Atonement. It seemed that it would be easier for a "camel to go through the eye of a needle" than for her to sincerely say, "I made a mistake, and I'm sorry."

If you knew there was an apology that would free your heart and mind from troubles or problems of the past or present, what would need to happen so you could offer or receive that apology?

One husband struggled to apologize to his wife and other family members. After a lifetime of lying, for him to take responsibility for his mistakes and lies was almost more than he could bear. He did everything he could to deny the need to apologize and then to delay apologizing. The beliefs that constrained him from apologizing included:

• A real man never apologizes.

• A good man is always right and therefore never needs to apologize.

• If I apologize, I will be less of a man.

• If I apologize, I will lose face with my wife. I am the head of my family, and I must always be seen as right if I am to have the respect I need and deserve.

• If I apologize, my wife will see my weaknesses. She will wish she had never married me.

The irony was that as he delayed apologizing, all the things that he feared would happen *if* he apologized actually happened *because* he didn't apologize. His wife and family lost more respect for him, and his weaknesses intensified in neon-like clarity.

Another irony was that his deepest desire, as he put it, was "to be the kind of man my sweetheart thought she married." However, self-deception held him captive. Lies ruled his life. He found himself lying about everything from finances to food. He continued to live far beneath his potential. His wife, a truth-seeker by nature who had become an exquisitely sensitive lie-detector, withdrew emotionally and physically from him. Her spirit was wounded by both his lies and the consequences of his lying. The more she withdrew, the more he tried to feign good-ness in order to be acceptable to her and draw her closer to him. She, of course, could detect his hypocrisy and withdrew even further.

Then one day this man looked into the mirror—not a man-made mirror, but the mirror of the Lord. He saw himself in stark reality. He saw the effects of his lies on himself, his wife, his mar-riage, and his family. And he came face to face with the meaning his wife attributed to his habit of lying.

He realized that, to his wife, his lies meant this: "I don't really love you or our children, and I don't really want to be with you through the eternities. I love these lies and self-deceptions more than I love you." He realized that the only way to break the grip that dishonesty had on him, his wife, and their marital intimacy was to speak the truth. It was the season to apologize.

He was fearful. Actually, he was almost immobilized by both his desire to finally speak the truth and his fear that he would make a mistake while apologizing. He began by putting his regrets and sorrows on paper; then he composed a letter of apol-ogy to his wife. After writing the first draft of the letter and let-ting it "cool" for a few days, he read it again, removing anything that sounded like an excuse, an explanation, or a rationalization for the things he had done.

It was very difficult for him to consistently take responsibil-ity for doing things that hurt his wife and their marriage. After years of providing explanations, which more often than not quickly turned into excuses, this man automatically rationalized his mistakes, missteps, and outright lies. Now, on bended knee, his knee-jerk reflex was no longer possible. Instead, he started saying to himself, "I will give up looking for why. I will keep looking for what I need to do—and do it!"

He found that before he could speak truth to others, he had to start speaking the truth to himself. He started coaching himself, telling himself that in order to counteract his lies of the past, he needed to be more bold in speaking the truth in the present. Many times he would remind himself:

• I will be bolder in declaring my sorrow for the grief I have caused my wife.

• I will be bolder in declaring that I have lived beneath myself, and I will avoid providing an explanation for why I did so.

• I will be clearer in thanking my wife, not just for staying with me but also for never giving up her vision of the man she deserves, the man I am coming to be.

• I will thank my wife for confronting me any time I appear to be cheating, lying, or not telling the whole truth.

The beliefs that began to help this man offer his apologies included:

• As the man of honor and the man of God I want to be, I need to be impeccably honest with myself and others.

• A good man is never taller than when kneeling in contrition for the mistakes he has made, especially when his mistakes have hurt others.

• A good man is able to say to the Lord, "I was wrong. What would you have me do?"

• A good man is never more right than when he is willing to apologize for his wrongs to those he has hurt.

• A man who is courageous in admitting his mistakes, lies, deceits, and problems of the past is freer to be his true self.

• When I apologize, my wife will have even more confidence in me because she will know I am telling the truth.

• When I apologize, my wife will be more drawn to me and to uniting her life with mine—because I will be more of who I really am.

Now, the challenge: How does a husband who has lied for years—and even lied about lying—win the trust of his wife sufficiently so that she really believes he is telling the truth when he finally apologizes? He worried that his wife would be like the woman in a cartoon whose husband pleads, "Carolyn, I wish you would tell me why you're upset with me. Whatever it is, I am very sorry! Please forgive—" The wife in the cartoon interrupts her husband: "How dare you apologize to me after what you did!"

Unfortunately, the man in our case example was right in assuming it would be difficult for his wife to accept his apology. Her constraining beliefs are typical of many:

• If I accept this apology, that means all of the anguish I've suffered because of my husband's behavior doesn't really matter. (As another woman said, weeping about the injustices perpetrated upon her: "Someone's got to pay for this!" Then she was reminded, "Someone already has—the Savior Himself.")

• If I accept this apology, my husband will just relax and go back to his old behavior. Only when I'm cold and punitive does he really try to live up to who he really is.

• I can accept his apology only when he has completely changed. He hasn't changed enough yet to warrant my accepting it.

Many husbands and wives are constrained from accepting their spouses' apologies because they believe, "I don't have to accept the apology of a bad, mean, or horrible person—not even when that person is my spouse!" However, our ways are not the Lord's ways. If we want to experience the God-given gift of marital intimacy, we need to live His ways. The Lord has set a high standard for us. He doesn't just say we need to accept the apology of bad, mean, or horrible people—He says we need to forgive them.

Forgiveness: An Integral Part of the Process

Many of us act as if forgiveness and repentance were only for the "righteous." It's almost as though we say, "Oh, she's a basically good person, therefore, I'll forgive her." But what about those who have caused us physical, emotional, mental, or spiritual suffering? What about those who have broken almost every commandment and covenant, bringing pain and conflict into our lives through their sinful choices? Do we have to forgive them? We do.

The Lord says, "I, the Lord, will forgive whom I will forgive, but of you it is required to forgive all men." (D&C 64:10.) Many people act as though this scripture reads in the reverse. They want to pick and choose whom they will forgive, based on their own standard of forgiveability. And their ultimate criterion seems to be that the sinner must suffer more than those who have suffered at the hands of the sinner.

What happens if we don't forgive others who have wronged us? The Lord is clear about the outcome: "If ye forgive men their trespasses your heavenly Father will also forgive you; But if ye forgive not men their trespasses neither will your Father forgive your trespasses." (3 Nephi 13:14–15.) He also explains an additional result of unforgiveness: "Ye ought to forgive one another; for he that forgiveth not his brother his trespasses standeth condemned before the Lord; for there remaineth in him the greater sin." (D&C 64:9.)

Could He possibly mean that by not forgiving someone who has harmed us, we become *more* sinful than the sinner? I believe the Lord is serious. He gave us His words because He means them. He has set a great example for us of saying what He means and meaning what He says.

The Lord's plea for us to give up hanging on to the sins of others in no way lessens the gravity of what the initial sinner did. As the Proclamation on the Family states, "We warn that individuals who violate covenants of chastity, who abuse spouse or offspring, or who fail to fulfill family responsibilities will one day stand accountable before God." But if we find ourselves drumming our fingers and saying to the sinner—either out loud or under our breath—"Your day will come," we may have a bit more work to do on forgiveness.

In D&C 64:8 the Lord tells us that we are to forgive one another *in our hearts.* Doesn't that speak to the depth of the forgiveness that we are to develop? The Lord doesn't say, "Forgive one another in your mouths." Perhaps that would just be saying words to the sinner, "I forgive you." And the Lord doesn't say, "Forgive one another in your minds." That would be like saying to ourselves, "Well, I forgive her." But to forgive in our hearts involves much more—a deep cleansing of the unforgiveness out of our hearts, even a change of heart.

That kind of forgiving is not easy. It is not something that happens overnight. It is something that can, depending on the gravity of the injustice, seem impossible at first. But it isn't impossible, or the Lord wouldn't have asked us to do it. (See 1 Nephi 3:7.) He has commanded us to forgive everyone! We need to find a way, and He will help us find the way if we ask.

The Lord doesn't seem to care "who started it." However, He does seem very concerned about getting rid of conflict between people. In fact, He is clear in telling us to be reconciled with others *before* coming unto Him: "If ye shall come unto me, or shall desire to come unto me, and rememberest that thy brother hath aught against thee—Go thy way unto thy brother, and first be reconciled to thy brother, and then come unto me with full purpose of heart, and I will receive you." (3 Nephi 12:23–24; see also Matthew 5:23–24.)

Is it true that we really can't see Him until we are reconciled with others? If you thought that a lack of forgiveness or apologies was keeping you from coming closer to the Savior, wouldn't you want to take care of that right now? One man from the depths of his humble heart said, "I am willing to do whatever it takes to have a great relationship with my wife." It took apologizing. Apologies that initially seemed humiliating to him were actually healing and strengthening, for him as well as for his wife. Following one apology he said, "I finally feel that the Savior really forgives me."

This man apologized to his wife's parents with his wife present as witness. Just before that apology, the husband and wife spoke about the wall that separated the two of them. His wife told him that there were about a hundred bricks in the wall, and that through this one apology to her parents he would take down twenty bricks! His motivation soared. And he succeeded in offering an apology to his in-laws, something he had been shrinking from for years.

There may be times that we need to offer what we would consider a "high-level" apology—some might even say an impossible apology. For example, President George Albert Smith offered such an apology to a man who spread false rumors about him, thus preventing him from becoming head of the Utah National Guard. President Smith was in anguish over this, filled with such an abundance of negative feelings that he even felt unworthy to partake of the Sacrament. His freedom from this suffering came when he went to the offending man and said, "I'm here to ask forgiveness for the hateful feelings I've had toward you." The other man, who was initially worried that George Albert Smith was going to physically annihilate him, became almost immediately apologetic himself, and the two became lifelong friends. (See Truman G. Madsen, *Presidents of the Church*, tape 8.)

Could it be that an apology to your spouse who has wronged you could free you both? In order to "lay aside every weight" and move ahead with your lives, you may need to say to your spouse who has hurt you: "I want to apologize for the negative feelings I've had about you," or, "I'm sorry I made you feel that you weren't even worthy of apologizing to me."

APOLOGIES WORTH
THEIR WEIGHT IN GOLD

There are other apologies that are worth their weight in gold and that refine the gold within the person apologizing. You are the voice of authority in many people's lives. You may not be giving yourself credit for the influence of your past actions and words, and for the healing effect of an apology from you. By apologizing, you can heal your spouse and your relationship in ways no one else can, and in the process you can become more of your true self. By apologizing, you can heal your children so that they can become better spouses. By apologizing, you can arise a bit more as a woman or man of God.

Any one of the following statements of apology spoken from the heart of a family member is worth at least ten sessions with the best counselor or therapist in the world. As one wife said to her husband, "Your loving words are worth all the Prozac money can buy!" Family members can heal each other like nothing else and no one else on earth. Consider the healing power in the following apologies:

A father to his son: "I'm so sorry that I didn't treat your mother better—showing her more love and respect—so that you would be more kind, more courageous, less easily discouraged, and therefore less easily frustrated in showing love to your own wife."

A mother to her daughter: "I'm sorry that I made your father feel so judged by me and deficient as a man. I'm sorry that my efforts to bring out the best in him only discouraged him and gave you a demeaning message about men."

A husband to his wife: "I'm sorry for the lust I brought to our marriage from pornographic magazines and movies that led me to explore other immoral activities. I'm so sorry that my increased lust decreased your trust in me."

A wife to her husband: "I'm sorry I made you feel that approaching me for marital intimacy was wrong. I'm sorry I didn't realize that marital intimacy can be sacred and sanctifying. Now I see that the very thing I've longed for—more spiritual and emotional connections with you—is possible through sexual intimacy which can unite us both physically and spiritually."

A father to his daughter: "I'm sorry I let anger rule our home. I'm sorry I thought I would be stronger and have more influence with anger as my companion. I'm sorry for the many times I wounded your spirit and made you doubt your worth as my daughter."

A mother to her son: "I'm sorry that you had to look to the world to learn about sex. It grieves me to think of the lies that the world and the adversary have sold you as 'truth' because I didn't teach you the eternal truths about marital intimacy."

A wife to her husband: "I'm sorry that despite all you have been through with disfellowshipment, working with the bishop through the difficult process of your repentance, and finally receiving full fellowship in the Church, that we're still not back into full fellowship with each other. I'm sorry that there are times when you feel like I haven't forgiven you and that sometimes this makes you wonder if the Savior has really forgiven you. I'm sorry that you constantly feel the need to prove yourself to me and that you doubt my love for you. I'm sorry that until recently when I really prayed about it, I couldn't understand the immense pull of your past addiction. I'm sorry that sometimes I forget how much you've been through—how much prayer, courage, and determination you've offered in order to triumph over the adversary. I'm sorry that I haven't told you often enough how much I love you and how proud I am of you—and how happy I am to be your wife."

A Broken Heart Helps Heal a Heart That Was Broken

The experience of one couple, Art and Lorraine, illustrates the healing power of apologies and forgiveness. The visualization exercise that helped them occurred after months of heart-to-heart conversations about the pain and suffering each of them had experienced, and months of repenting, apologizing, and forgiving.

Art longed to do anything he could do in order to heal Lorraine's heart, which he had wounded over and over again during their twenty-five years of marriage. In his effort to take responsibility for the pain he had caused her, he brought his broken heart and contrite spirit to her and to the Lord. Strengthened by the Lord, he willingly listened at length to the embarrassment, shame, turmoil, anguish, and despair Lorraine had experienced because of his mistakes, missteps, and sins. Several weeks later, he helped her visualize a variety of healing images, the most powerful of which came to her mind as he spoke the following words, paced to allow time for Lorraine to picture the image, reflect on it, and respond as she desired.

"Picture the Savior embracing you. Picture Him telling you that you've done a great job, that He's pleased with you, that He loves you. Can you picture that?

"Tell me anything you want about that image of being held lovingly by the Savior. You are indeed one of His valiant daughters. He loves you. And I love you.

"Now picture me walking into that scene. Picture the Savior smiling at us and saying, 'You and Art have an important work to do together. One of the important things you will do is to learn about love together.'

"Picture the Savior teaching us about the Atonement—and about its power to heal the pain I caused you. Can you hear what He's saying? Tell me. [He knew that Lorraine had a marvelous ability to hear the voice of the Lord.] What does He want us to know?

"Can you hear Him telling us about what we need to do next in order to gain access to even more of the power in the Atonement so that your pain, which I caused, will be healed? What does He want us to do? What does He want us to say? Can you hear the Savior giving me counsel about how I should treat you? What is He saying?

"Now, picture the three of us talking about the truths of marital intimacy. Take your time. What do you hear or see?

"Now, picture you and me looking at each other, as Adam and Eve did, and saying that we are willing to learn about love together. Picture that in that moment we know the beauty, the tenderness, the sanctity, the strength, the purified excitement, and the soul-expanding love that occurs when you and I—within the covenant of marriage—partake of true marital intimacy.

"We knew we would have obstacles. We knew we loved each other deeply. And we knew that with the power and love of the Savior's atonement, we could and would succeed.

"I do love you."

Chapter 8

LEARNING A NEW LANGUAGE
OF MARITAL INTIMACY

W hat's in a name? Does it really matter what you call
something? Consider this: Is it more appealing to eat
"snails" or "escargots"? A change in words can free
us—free our thoughts, our actions, and our feelings.

Words do not come unattached. They trail beliefs and para-
digms. Unfortunately, the world has brutalized and plagiarized
the words "sex" and "love"—and almost every word or phrase
related to those words—and has, at the same time, sexualized
almost everything in the world. The world's words about
love and sex come trailing the world's views. When we use the
world's words, those words invite us to see things through
the world's lens, and we can become trapped in the world's ideas
about intimacy.

One way to come out from the influence of the world, and
therefore to be more open to truths about intimacy, is to be careful with our language about this most sacred of topics.

Words and phrases such as *fool around* and *mess around* do not describe the sacred process of marital intimacy, nor do they give it the dignity it deserves. These terms imply that physical union is nothing more than a game, something with which to "play around." While sexual intimacy can be enjoyable in every respect, and yes, even fun, it is so much more than that. It is a marvelous gift given by God exclusively to husbands and wives to enjoy, in order to draw closer to each other and to Him, to create love and power, joy and peace, as well as bodies for our Heavenly Father's children.

Having sex and *making love* are phrases we've inherited from the world that perpetuate the paradigm of the world. *Having sex* can be defined as a sexual uniting and physiological release of hormones, and perhaps tension, between two individuals. *Making love* in a worldly sense can be defined, at best, as a loving, physically intimate exchange between two consenting adults—though no consideration is given to gender, marital status, or to one's spirit.

The Apostle Paul invites us to be unconstrained by the world—to leave the words, views, and wisdom of the world behind: "Be not conformed to this world: but be ye transformed by the renewing of your mind, that ye may prove what is that good, and acceptable, and perfect, will of God." (Romans 12:2.)

When we use language different from that of the world to consider and discuss spiritual truths about physical intimacy, our minds *will* be renewed and transformed, and we will not be conformed to the world. By doing so we can come to understand the "good, and acceptable, and perfect, will of God" about our marital intimacy. Learning a new language of marital intimacy can be liberating!

With this in mind, would the term *co-creating love* move us away from the world's view and into a new paradigm about intimacy? Perhaps *co-creating love* can bring to our minds the great need for both spouses to feel more loved, more adored, and more respected before, during, and after their sacred uniting. Perhaps *co-creating love* can help us remember that this exclusive, love-generating experience can really happen only when a husband and wife worthily join their bodies *and* their spirits. Perhaps *co-creating love* can stretch our minds to consider how the experience unifies and unites spouses as nothing else can— how it heals each spouse's spirit and lifts each spouse's sights to the eternal possibilities of their relationship and lives.

Perhaps *co-creating love* can invite us to remember that love and joy and light and truth and power and peace are eternal companions, and that when spouses co-create pure love, they also co-create joy and light and truth and power and peace in their relationship.

Perhaps *co-creating love* can help take us out of the world and help us draw a larger distinction between how the world views "having sex" and "making love," and how we as men and women of God view and experience intimacy that is not of this world. Perhaps the term *co-creating love* can bring to our understanding the truth that true marital intimacy results in drawing spouses closer to God, the creator and source of true love.

And what word might describe the anticipatory activities that prepare couples for co-creating love? The word presently used by the world once again sends the message that sexual intimacy is just a game. Perhaps the word *prelude* more nearly captures the experiences that precede and are part of the kind of physical intimacy spouses-of-covenant long to experience. Think of what prelude music does: it sets the stage for what is to follow and invites the listener to want more. In worship services, the prelude music is pivotal to inviting the Spirit, inviting us out of the world, away from our cares and worries. The word *prelude* seems consistent with the gospel lens of marital intimacy.

CO-CREATING LOVE WITHIN COVENANTS

As Latter-day Saints, we have made and are striving daily to keep sacred covenants with the Lord. Because of these covenants, Latter-day Saint spouses can experience marital intimacy that is different from, and even more satisfying than, the kind of "intimacy" celebrated and depicted by the world.

As Latter-day Saints we are trying to be a godly people, walking in all holiness before the Lord. Therefore, we can't compartmentalize our lives. We can't live as men and women of God in all areas of life except that of sexual relations. We can't expect to turn our sexual lives over to the adversary—even in the subtleties of our language, and more importantly in our behavior—and not expect to become, at least when it comes to love and sex, men and women of the world.

The good news is that as we turn away from the language of the world, the false images and lies about love and sex can begin to fade. Two possibilities as part of a new language of love have been offered in this chapter: *co-creating love* and *prelude*. Neither of these possibilities may be a fit for you, but perhaps just thinking about them can open your mind to words and phrases that will help you not be constrained by the world's words, and therefore its views, of marital intimacy.

As we come out of the world by using language that is consistent with gospel truths about intimacy, we can have marriage and family relationships that are not *of* this world. Latter-day Saint couples can experience more than temple weddings; they can more fully embrace the joys of temple marriages. And they can commence the process that culminates in truly *co-creating love*.

PART 4

ETERNAL TRUTHS ABOUT MARITAL INTIMACY

*What would you want to do if you discovered that
many of the plain and precious truths about
sexual intimacy that have been lost
by the world have been revealed
through the restored gospel of Jesus Christ?*

Three of those eternal truths about marital intimacy are:
1. Soulful joining brings joy.
2. Unity is power.
3. Sacred intimacy can be sanctifying.

Chapter 9

SOULFUL JOINING
BRINGS JOY

As Latter-day Saints we are doctrinally distinct in understanding that the body and spirit constitute the soul. (D&C 88:15; see also James E. Talmage, in Conference Report, October 1913, 117.) That one gospel truth alone can open our eyes, minds, and hearts to thinking about life and love and intimacy in a whole new way.

ETERNAL TRUTHS VERSUS
WORLDLY BELIEFS

How distinct and different are eternal truths from the beliefs offered by most of the world?

Much of the world would have us believe there is no God, no devil, and no need for a Redeemer because there is no right or wrong—and certainly no sin or penalties. Most would like to convince us that we are basically like animals, ruled by appetites and passions—which, unless satisfied, will lead to emotional, mental, and even physical disturbances and distress. Many believe that the body is the bane of our existence, something to put up with until we die and are freed from it. Others see the body as a toy, something to help us live by the credo "Eat, drink, and be merry, for tomorrow we die." (2 Nephi 28:7.) And to the world, the soul is the spirit, and the spirit is the soul—period.

What difference does truth make in our lives? Imagine how deeply grateful we were premortally for the plan of salvation and happiness that provided a Savior to pay the price for our sins. How thankful we must have been that Jesus Christ would redeem us from physical death (the separation of our bodies from our spirits) and from spiritual death (our separation from God due to sin).

Perhaps we reviewed our "things to do on Earth" list over and over again, hoping that we would never forget our premortal commitments despite the veil that would be placed over our minds. We knew that the Holy Ghost, a member of the Godhead, would bring all things to our remembrance (see John 14:26) as we lived worthily and sought for His guidance and direction. What a comfort it must have been to know we would have the gift of the Holy Ghost!

So, we may have thought, just how difficult could earth life be?

We knew who we were:
• Children of God.

We knew what that meant:
• We had divine characteristics and abilities.

We knew how to communicate with our Heavenly Father:
• Ask Him with a sincere heart and real intent in the name of Jesus Christ, with faith in Him, doubting nothing.

We knew how to listen to the voice of the Lord:
• Be open to the still, small voice, the whisperings of the Holy Ghost, who would speak to our minds and hearts as we

immersed ourselves in prayer, the scriptures, and temple worship.

• Listen to the prophets, seers, and revelators of God.

Heavenly parents. A premortal life. A Redeemer. The companionship of the Holy Ghost to guide us. What do these eternal truths have to do with marital intimacy? What's the connection?

Three Truths about the Soul

Think about these three doctrinal truths related to your soul:

1. Your body is the great prize of mortal life.

2. Your body and your spirit constitute your soul.

3. When your body and spirit are separated, you cannot have a fulness of joy.

Let's consider the implications of each of these soul-related truths for your marriage.

1. Your body is the great prize of mortal life.

We are the spirit offspring of God! We lived as spirit children with our heavenly parents for eons, learning truths and developing our abilities. One of the great reasons for our mortal sojourn was to receive the gift of a body, which would move us forward in our progression. The Prophet Joseph Smith declared: "We came to this earth that we might have a body and present it pure before God in the celestial kingdom. The great principle of happiness consists in having a body. The devil has no body, and herein is his punishment." (*Teachings of the Prophet Joseph Smith,* 181.) It really is true: our bodies are a merited gift, "the sign of our royal birthright" (James E. Talmage, in Conference Report, October 1913, 117), even "the temple of the Holy Ghost" (1 Corinthians 6:19).

Satan desires control over our bodies, and goes to extraordinary lengths to coerce us into relinquishing that control. Because he doesn't have a body, he is presumably particularly covetous of ours. He rejoices when we believe lies about how to use, feed, and even clothe them. He tries relentlessly to have us abuse our bodies or those of others. In these and countless other ways he seeks to entice us to give him control.

The truth is that our spirits are to control our bodies. Brigham Young gave this counsel: "If the spirit yields to the body, it becomes corrupt; but if the body yields to the spirit, it becomes pure and holy." (*Discourses of Brigham Young*, 267.) Sobering though it may be to contemplate, when we overeat or undereat, overexercise or underexercise, become obsessed with our bodies or neglect our bodies, we may be slowly relinquishing control of our bodies to Satan—as our spirits increasingly lose control. No wonder Brigham Young also taught, "You cannot inherit eternal life, unless your appetites are brought in subjection to the spirit that lives within you, that spirit which our Father in Heaven gave. . . . The tabernacles must be brought in subjection to the spirit perfectly; or your bodies cannot be raised to inherit eternal life." (*Discourses of Brigham Young*, 266.)

Considering the connection between the influence of one's spirit over one's body and the amount of joy possible, one woman started to wonder if one of the most important things she could do to experience more joy in sexual intimacy would be to strengthen her spirit so that it could influence her body more. She started to think about exercising and healthy eating as ways to increase her spirit's influence on her body. She began to view the Word of Wisdom as a marital intimacy gift from her Father in heaven to help her. Over time, her diligence and heed in following the Lord's law of health dramatically increased, and her sexual fulfillment followed.

2. Your body and your spirit constitute your soul.

In latter-day revelation, the Lord teaches us about the connection between our bodies and our spirits: "The *spirit and the body* are the soul of man." (D&C 88:15; emphasis added.) Doesn't the messenger, the Savior Himself, add to the weight of the message? The very One who bought our souls—our bodies and spirits—teaches us about them! The Lord knows the truth. Our bodies and spirits, our souls, are His. His pure, atoning blood paid for them.

If husbands and wives wish to co-create true, joy-filled love, their souls—bodies *and* spirits—must be clean when they unite. This requirement explains why the adversary is so clever in enticing us with what one couple called "lust dust" designed to soil and denigrate our spirits. This couple found that things improved in their marital intimacy when they regularly examined how clean their spirits were. They looked for ways that Satan was subtly—and sometimes not so subtly—soiling their spirits and their home. In a spirit of searching together, rather than blaming each other, they looked for "lust-dust bunnies" in their bedroom and checked for "lust-dust mites" in their minds. They were amazed at what they found when they were willing to seek. For example, the wife found "lust dust" attached to her previously favorite, although very worldly, negligee that she now felt was not appropriate for a woman of covenant to wear. The husband found "lust dust" in several of his fitness and sports magazines, which he then discontinued his subscriptions to. The couple continued to seek, find, and remove anything that was contaminating their spirits and thus constraining their intimacy. This honest and ongoing process drew their hearts out to one another, securing a boundary around their marriage that had been lacking before.

This couple also took great care in bringing clean bodies to their moments of marital intimacy. As basic as it sounds, they discovered that remembering that their bodies are part of their souls caused them to take a little more care with their personal hygiene. They wanted to do everything they could to have their marital intimacy be a soulful experience, and that included properly cleansing their bodies.

3. When your body and spirit are separated, you cannot have a fulness of joy.

In Doctrine and Covenants 93:33–34 the Lord teaches that when our bodies and spirits are "inseparably connected, [we] receive a fulness of joy; and when separated, [we] cannot receive a fulness of joy."

What a profound truth! We know that ultimately that

statement refers to the need for the resurrection and to the fulness of joy we will experience when our bodies and spirits are reunited after death. But could that truth also help us understand why far too many couples are not finding more joy in marital intimacy? Bodies *and* spirits need to be united for joy to occur. We know that "the dead . . . [look] upon the long absence of their spirits from their bodies as a bondage." (D&C 138:50.) Many couples feel like they are in bondage to lifeless, loveless marriages where only bodies unite from time to time.

Elder Jeffrey R. Holland taught that sexual intimacy is to be a union of souls. (See "Of Souls, Symbols, and Sacraments," 162.) Could it be that you are not finding more joy in your marital intimacy because your body *and* spirit are not uniting with the body *and* spirit of your spouse? If you focus only on the uniting of your bodies, you will miss much of the joy marital intimacy can bring. So, how can husbands and wives ensure that their spirits as well as their bodies are joined together?

YOUR WHOLE SOUL

True marital intimacy requires that your body *and* spirit be fully present. For example, if your mind is on your worries at work and your heart is filled with anger toward your spouse, sexual union may occur, but sexual intimacy cannot. Therefore, it is important to identify anything that may be preventing your whole soul from being completely engaged with your spouse's.

One woman said, "My husband yells at me throughout the day or gives me the cold shoulder and then wants to be intimately close at night. Well, he may have my body, but he'll never have my whole soul." When her husband realized the consequences of his punitive behavior, his desire to change increased tenfold. He and his wife started talking about what each of them could do so they wouldn't feel so lonely and rejected. They started talking more and sharing what was on their minds and in their hearts. And they started to be kind.

Over time, they began to notice that their marital intimacy was much improved when more of each spouse's spirit was present in their physical relationship. "I really focus on 'us' now when we're intimate," the wife said. "I no longer feel that I need to hold back and protect myself. My spirit feels safe with my husband for the first time in our marriage." The husband concurred: "I didn't think it was going to be possible after all these years, but when our whole souls unite during sexual intimacy, I give my love differently to my wife and she receives it differently."

Much has been written about the differences between men and women—in how they show love, want to receive love, communicate verbally and nonverbally, respond physiologically—and the list goes on. But the great cross-gender, cross-culture, cross-creed truth is that physical intimacy at its best is a soulful experience—an experience that involves the spirit and the body. And when physical intimacy is soulful it is joyful—for both spouses!

On initially hearing the "soulful truth," some have asked, almost in amazement, "How can sex involve my spirit? How can sexual intimacy be a spiritual experience?" Perhaps the real question should be, "How can co-creating love *not* be a spiritual experience?" Consider what we know:

• Marital intimacy was given by God exclusively for His children who are husbands and wives.

• Marital intimacy carries with it procreative power—the power to give life to another spirit child of God, and to give life to each spouse and to their relationship.

How could an experience with such profound facets *not* be directly connected to our spirits—and to *the* Spirit?

WANTED: MORE JOY!

Joy arises in marital intimacy as soul is intertwined with soul. The more "soulful" the coming together, the more joyful the experience. And it is also true that the less "soulful" the experience, the less joyful it will be.

If physical intimacy consists only of the joining of bodies, or involves the joining of bodies and of wounded spirits, marital intimacy will not be as joyful. It is that simple. It may be pleasurable in the moment, but in most cases even that will not occur.

On considering the grand truth that physical intimacy is to be a soulful experience, one couple talked about what had constrained each of them from bringing both their bodies *and* their spirits to their efforts to co-create love. They realized that because of sin and sorrow, self-deprecation and self-absorption, what they had joined together on their wedding night—and for the majority of many years of nights following—were two bodies and two wounded, weak spirits.

As the years unfolded, this husband and wife continued to be attracted to each other physically but not spiritually. She doubted his spiritual strength and maturity, and he always felt as though he was less than he should be in her presence. He experienced her spirit as controlling, condescending, and emasculating. Their lives continued on ever-separating paths.

FROM SPIRITUAL IMPOTENCE
TO SPIRITUAL POTENCY

When this husband was introduced to the idea of marital intimacy as a soulful experience, he found it intriguing and energizing. He started to shift from his immobilizing, impotent feeling of "There is nothing I can do that will make a difference; my wife will never want to make love with me" to a position of "I am willing to try something different. I want to do this. I can do this." His willingness to think about the soulful nature of true intimacy and its implications for his marriage brought hope back to his heart and mind.

Thinking about co-creating love as a time to join his body with his wife's body and his spirit with hers gave him a whole new perspective on intimacy and on those things that fortified his spirit. Spiritually strengthening activities were now *his* choice, his idea, part of his efforts to improve the intimate times he shared with his wife.

This man had always felt very protective of his agency—especially where his wife was concerned. He and his wife were caught in a vicious cycle they had created together where the more she asked him to do something spiritual, the less likely he was to do it. He was like another man who said, "I read my scriptures at work so that my wife doesn't know. I don't want to give her the satisfaction that I'm doing what *she* wants me to do." Both of these men heard their wives' requests for spiritually strengthening activities not as invitations to be true to themselves, but as commands and demands, which sent the message, "I won't love you unless you . . ." and "You are inadequate because you don't . . ."

This husband acknowledged that stubborn pride had prevented him from doing the very things he knew he should do. He admitted, "Sometimes I find myself saying defiantly to my wife: 'I'm not going to read my scriptures and pray just because you want me to' and 'I'll watch what I want to watch on TV, when I want to watch it!' At those times I now realize I've been pushing myself into a corner, and reducing my degrees of freedom much more than my wife ever did."

It started to make sense to him that if he brought only his body to bed and did nothing about the condition of his spirit, both his and his wife's desires for marital intimacy could never really be met. He started to think about how he could bring his "personal-best spirit" to their physical unions. He started to think in an entirely different way about praying, scripture reading, keeping the Sabbath day holy, and avoiding questionable or worldly television and movies. No longer were these things to do to appease his wife or keep the bishop off his back. Rather, these were now things he could do to bring his spirit back to life, so that he could bring his body and his spirit to their relationship and enjoy intimacy on many levels.

Continued deep reflection on this soulful truth brought this husband's spirit more life, confidence, and joy than he had known in many years. He found himself eager to do whatever it took to work with the Lord in resuscitating his spirit and strengthening himself spiritually. He wanted to do his part so that he and his wife could experience the joys associated with this great gift of love.

JOYFUL SATISFACTION: THE JOINING OF BODY AND SPIRIT

One couple found themselves caught in a demoralizing cycle in which the wife felt frustrated by her husband's advances and he felt that he was always begging her for physical contact. Each of them felt a loneliness that was almost palpable. The only way this couple ever momentarily stopped the cycle of his pursuing and her withdrawing was when the wife would "give in."

They were each so lonely and unhappy because, rather than co-creating love, they were participating in sex that gratifies but never satisfies. This kind of physical relationship conjures up the image of a baby pacifier. Baby pacifiers are used to keep fussy babies quiet. Pacifiers don't solve the problem of why the baby is crying, they simply keep the baby quiet and temporarily happy. Baby pacifiers don't really nourish or nurture.

In the case of the husband and wife mentioned above, their physical intimacy was little more than a pacifier. No wonder they were not sexually fulfilled. Following their participation in imitations of true marital intimacy, the husband was usually even more frustrated, and even more likely to treat his wife as an object of lust in a misguided effort to experience real love.

Let's consider another reason why this couple suffered so much. When the wife "gave in," she demeaned both her husband and herself. How? She demeaned her husband by her thoughts about him: "Big baby. I'll just give him something to keep him quiet." She demeaned herself by her actions, which basically said to her husband and to herself, "Here's my body. Do with it what you will!" This is hardly the attitude of a woman who appreciates that her body is the great prize of life.

Things started to change when the wife realized that she could stop feeling like a "thing" and begin feeling like a whole woman as she *chose* to offer her whole soul—her whole spirit and her whole body—to her husband. "When I realize it's *my* choice," she said, "that seems to make all the difference. It's my body and my spirit. When I choose to give them to my husband, I feel love for my husband and from him. I love my husband, but I've been running away from his advances. But now, when I realize the vicious cycle we've been stuck in, and my part in keeping that cycle going, I want to do my part in stopping it. I want to co-create love with my husband so that each of us feels more loved afterward. What a difference that will be! Now I know how to bring my whole soul to our intimate relationship. It's my choice."

Another wife realized that engaging in sex that gratifies but never satisfies was contributing to her physical exhaustion. "I always thought I was 'just too tired for sex,'" she said. "We have five children, and I'm busy. I really am tired by the end of the day. But when my husband and I started joining our bodies *and* our spirits—not just our bodies—I noticed that I started feeling different. Soulful marital intimacy seemed to energize my spirit, and my body followed. Now, at the end of an exhausting day, I love being with my husband. It nourishes my body and my spirit. For me, co-creating love is the perfect ending to an overwhelming day."

Each spouse has a responsibility to bring the brightest, best, largest spirit to their relationship so that their experiences are so much more than just "sexual union"—that they are truly times of co-creating love.

When you remember that
• your body is the great prize of life
and that
• your body and your spirit constitute your soul
and that

• when your body and your spirit are separated there cannot be a fulness of joy

and that

• marital intimacy is to be a soulful experience

and that

• marital intimacy unites the soul (which is the body and spirit) of the husband with the soul (the body and spirit) of the wife

then . . . there is joy!

QUESTIONS TO CONSIDER

• What would need to be different in your marriage for you and your spouse to begin to experience physical intimacy as a more soulful experience—an experience where both your bodies and spirits are more united?

• What can you do to show that you believe that your body is the great prize of life?

• What would help your spirit feel more alive so that you would have even more to bring to your sexual intimacy?

• Do you know what nurtures, enlarges, and brightens your spouse's spirit?

Chapter 10

UNITY
IS POWER

True marital intimacy, very simply but very significantly, is a symbolic experience reserved exclusively for thoroughly united husbands and wives that brings them joy, love, peace, and power.

The possibility of such fulfillment is available to all who desire it. It is real. Passion that is purified and therefore powerful can occur when your physical union is a symbol of the total uniting of your lives.

A young couple, parents of two small children, wrote eloquently of their experiences with true marital intimacy: "Intimacy comprises two hearts being turned toward each other twenty-four hours a day. Intimacy is a longing to share or connect with the experience of the other through invitation, patience, long-suffering, sacrifice, and open expressions of love. When several smaller intimate moments have been enjoyed between us, it makes the ultimate outward act of love longed for and so much more special. The physical union is actually a blending of the physical, emotional, psychological, and spiritual sensations that make up the love we have for one another."

What if, before you and your spouse commenced co-creating love, a measuring device registered how united your hearts were and prevented sexual union unless you wanted to unite everything in your lives? How quickly would some of your old habits—your inability to communicate, your unkind words, your self-absorption—fall away?

Your physical uniting is to be a symbol of your total union, not the only occurrence of union in your marriage. (See Holland, "Of Souls, Symbols, and Sacraments," 158.) It should represent the complete merger of your hearts, dreams, and desires. It should be not only a physical merger but an emotional and spiritual one as well. This concept stands in stark contrast to the media's portrayal of "love" and "romance," in which couples meet and engage in sexual activities well outside the complete merging of their lives within marriage.

UNITY AND POWER

When marital intimacy is a symbol of the total union of a husband and wife, the benefits abound. Total union involves union of feeling. Said the Prophet Joseph Smith, "By union of feeling we obtain power with God." (*Discourses of the Prophet Joseph Smith*, 88.) Imagine what power is available as husbands and wives become more and more united—united in every respect. Power with God to bless their lives and their families! And conversely, imagine what power remains untapped when husbands and wives are not united.

The adversary knows the power, the sanctity, and the uniqueness of marital intimacy. Thus, he works to keep spouses from thinking about the sustaining, life-giving power that flows from this most sacred of unions. He seeks to blind spouses to that truth by perpetuating images and messages in numerous forums that focus only on the physical act. He doesn't want couples to think about what it really means to be joined together in all aspects of their lives. He doesn't want husbands and wives to ask their Heavenly Father about the power available to them and their marriage as they keep the law of chastity with exquisite precision and as they unite their lives in ever-increasing ways.

BECOMING ONE:
BIOLOGICALLY SPEAKING

What happens as spouses become more and more united in their daily lives? The science of biology has an interesting answer. A biological principle called "structural coupling" describes what happens when two entities have repeated and recurring interactions with each other. Each interaction between the two triggers changes. Over time, through repeated interactions, these two distinct entities become less different from each other and more alike. There is an increasingly better "fit." Like feet and shoes, like two stones rubbed together, they change as they interact. (See Maturana and Varela, *The Tree of Knowledge*.)

When we interact with someone or something repeatedly over time, we change. We become more and more like the person or thing, the idea or the image with which we spend more and more time. Our cells change. Our souls change. Our countenances change.

"Structural coupling" explains why some couples begin to look like each other, why friends begin to dress and talk alike, why colleagues reach the point where they can finish each other's sentences. The more people interact, the more united they are, the more they become "one." The Father and the Son are the ultimate example of this principle.

We are complex, multifaceted beings who are constantly changing. Our various facets are physical, psychological, social, and spiritual—each of which is influenced by the other facets as we grow and develop. What we are able to experience in life— to see, hear, feel, think, and so on—depends on the state of the development and health of these many aspects of our selves.

A biological experiment involved rotating a frog's eye 180 degrees. The researchers were surprised to discover that the image of a worm was *transformed*, not transmitted, by the frog's eye, as originally thought. What they learned was that what the frog saw when "looking at" a worm was determined by the internal structure of the frog's eye, not by the external stimulus of the worm. A song from the early '70s says, "A man hears what he wants to hear and disregards the rest." With apologies to Simon and Garfunkel, we could say, "A man hears what he is able to hear, as determined by his present development, and doesn't know that he is disregarding the rest." And the same is true, of course, for a woman.

We have all experienced the effect of our current physical, psychological, social, and spiritual state on our ability to hear and see. We read a scripture one day and see and understand certain things. A few days later we read the same scripture and see something new and understand something different. This happens because *we* are different. The intervening experiences we've had, even in just a few days, have changed us in some way. As Robert L. Millet, former dean of Religious Education at Brigham Young University, has said, "Most of the time we do not see things as they really are; we see things as we really are." (*Alive in Christ*, 29.)

As spouses have more and more experiences together, changes occur in each of them, in concert with the other. Their interactions trigger physical and spiritual changes in both of them. The more they interact with each other, the more alike they become. They start looking and seeing like each other. And they become increasingly united.

BECOMING ONE:
SOCIOLOGICALLY SPEAKING

What else happens as a husband and wife intertwine their lives? A sociological principle teaches that increased interaction leads to increased sentiment. It stands to reason that the more that spouses interact with each other, the more feelings they will have for each other. The less they interact with each other, the fewer feelings they will have for each other. Obviously, there are many ways to have increased interaction. It is possible to be on different continents but to still interact because you are thinking about the other person and mindful of his or her activities and well-being—and your heart is drawn out to that person. On the other hand, if you are interacting with others and never thinking of your spouse, the truism will hold: Absence makes the heart grow fonder—for somebody else!

One young husband, watching the dying embers of his relationship with his wife, reflected on their heartbreaking situation and wrote these words of wisdom: "My wife and I have been married for about eighteen months. She and I will be the first to admit that we have had our difficulties and trials in trying to have a successful marriage. Our temple sealer told us that our marriage would never work if we would not look into the mirror together (figuratively speaking). We never did, and that led to a lot of pain and suffering for both of us."

Shortly thereafter they divorced. His wife had developed a close relationship with a co-worker, her "best friend." Best friends are people with whom you do things, with whom you share your thoughts, feelings, dreams, and desires. She had done all of that with her male co-worker, and the increased interaction had led to deeper feelings for him. No wonder President Gordon B. Hinckley has cautioned men and women who work together, "Do your job, but keep your distance." (*Ensign*, November 1998, 98.) The more the wife shared with her co-worker, the less she shared with her husband. Decreased interaction with her husband decreased her feelings for him—and decreased her desire to "look into the mirror" with him.

Where do you spend your time? With whom do you interact? Most couples find that their marriages suffer when the wife is "married" to her children (and they do indeed become "her" children, not "theirs") or the husband is "married" to his career.

If the only time a husband and wife unite is during physical union, true marital intimacy is not possible. Instead, the couple is probably experiencing "counterfeit intimacy," as Victor L. Brown Jr. described it. (*Human Intimacy,* 5.) "Counterfeit intimacy" occurs when we relate to each other in fragments—a fragment of a wife here connecting with a fragment of her husband there.

With just those two principles in mind—one from biology, one from sociology—we can begin to understand why it is so important that spouses share experiences of many kinds with each other so that their physical intimacy is truly a symbol of how united their lives are.

BECOMING ONE THROUGH THOUGHTS, ACTIONS, AND WORDS

When spouses are truly one, anything done for one is really done for the other. They are a unit. There is no *his* and *hers;* rather *we, us,* and *ours* become the operative words. Even activities done individually don't feel separate when spouses are united in their hearts and minds.

When couples are united in everything, there are no arguments about who is giving 51 percent and who is giving 49. One couple realized that when they found themselves asking, "What am I willing to give so I can get what I want out of this marriage?" they were already on their way "out of" their marriage. They also discovered that when they worried about reciprocity ("Unless I get back exactly what I give, I'm out of here"), they weren't really "in" their marriage. It was only as they started to remember their covenants with the Lord and each other, as they started to think of their marriage as a living, growing entity that was "theirs," that things started to change dramatically. Each spouse stopped thinking, "I did that for my spouse; now what is my spouse going to do for me?" and started thinking, "I did that for us, to help our marriage grow. What else can I do?"

Each spouse began to see that as the marriage went, so went his or her own happiness. In the early stages of this change, they started a friendly, almost comical, competition to see who could do the most to help their marriage grow. They discovered the wonderful economy of becoming more united: Anything they did to help their marriage also helped them individually.

Thinking about marital intimacy as a symbol of total intimacy lifts our sights. Questions that constrain marital intimacy, such as "What's in this relationship for me?" "What has my spouse done for me lately?" or "Why do I always have to be the one who is willing to change and to sacrifice for the good of our marriage?" shift to questions that improve marital intimacy: "What can I do to show more love to my spouse?" "What else can I do to strengthen our relationship?" and "How can we become even more united, emotionally and spiritually as well as physically?"

When spouses catch the vision of what it means to become one—outside as well as inside the bedroom—their language and behavior change. Think about how differently your day might unfold, how differently you might experience your daily activities, and even how different your "to-do" list might look if you did everything with two people in mind: the Savior and your spouse. Imagine how the drudgery of some tasks would diminish if you thought, "I am doing this to help strengthen my marriage and build the Kingdom." Think about how the heaviness of some challenges would lift if you really believed, "I am doing this for the good of my marriage and for the Lord."

It's about Time

One husband discovered that he became much more mindful of and creative in involving his wife in his life when he focused on being totally united with her. He realized that, even as busy as they were, they could find many opportunities to do things together so that she would feel his devotion to her and their marriage. They moved their desks from separate rooms into one larger room so they could be near each other even when they were both mired in work. He said it made them feel that they were working "shoulder to shoulder." They found this closeness to be a great comfort, and it reduced the stress they felt when deadlines on projects were looming. In addition, the memory of working side-by-side was comforting when later assignments prevented them from spending as much time together.

You may be thinking, "But I can't do my work with my spouse in the same room," or "We don't have any more minutes in our day to do anything together." Perhaps you can appreciate the situation of the husband and wife who had been "married" for thirty years. They sought help for their failing relationship. A successful entrepreneur, the husband had created and sold several international companies. The wife was a teacher who enjoyed her days of stimulating bright young minds now that their own children were in high school. These two people (they weren't really a couple at that point) were living fully their individual lives. They came to therapy wondering if they were really capable of having a marriage, or if they should "cut their losses" and divorce.

To live separately and singly within marriage is a travesty. It wounds and depresses each spouse's spirit because it's wrong! It's not the way "marriage" is supposed to be. When spouses feel alone in their marriage, they can't bring their whole souls to their sexual unions, and thus their sexual unions are only physical experiences. That was the case with this man and woman. Their sexual unions were indeed symbolic—symbolic of the poverty of their experiences together. An assignment from their therapist helped them discover a simple yet powerful solution to their loneliness and dissatisfaction. They were asked to spend fifteen minutes a day talking about any one of the following topics: "I feel sad/mad/bad/glad about . . ." One day one spouse was to talk while the other listened. The next day they were to switch.

Two weeks later, the spouses returned to report to the therapist. With a mixture of relief and horror, the husband said, "We've found the problem. We tried to do the assignment. And guess what? We couldn't do it. We don't even take fifteen minutes a day to talk together! We know what to do now." They committed to taking time daily to be with each other, to talk with each other, to learn from and grow with each other. They were committed in an entirely different way to uniting and being one.

Even small increases in time together can greatly improve marital intimacy. Consider the following experience of a husband who felt numb from years of feeling unloved and sexually rejected by his wife. He was amazed at what happened when they started increasing their time together, even in seemingly small ways. He wrote: "In the past week or so I have been skeptical and cautious about feeling anything. I've been surprised at what a difference reading scriptures together, reading a book on marital intimacy together, and praying together have made! At times, I've noticed strong feelings of love for my wife, especially when we've been reading."

UNITY IS MORE THAN DOING THINGS TOGETHER

The unity that undergirds marital intimacy requires a husband and wife to do more than just share activities. Doing things with your spouse is a necessary but not sufficient condition for the kind of total unity that allows spouses to truly co-create love.

This became painfully clear to a couple who were engaged to be married. Diane and Robert had known each other for three years and had broken up several times. Diane discovered that although she and her betrothed had spent many hours together and enjoyed doing things together, they really didn't have a relationship on which to build a strong marriage.

Diane loved Robert. He was a good man with great qualities, and she had a profound respect for him. Yet she couldn't sustain her desire to marry him. The closer the date for their marriage came, the more her tears and fears increased. When asked how Robert responded when she talked with him about things dear to her heart, her response was, "Oh, I don't talk with him about *that.* He might feel bad or get upset. Usually when I tell him about things that mean a lot to me, he hardly responds or tells me that I'm making too much of an issue out of it—and then I feel worse."

Diane withheld her heartfelt desires and emotions from Robert, believing that her husband-to-be might not like them and, therefore, not like her. Her withholding of information and Robert's negation of her feelings kept them from being unified. Diane also began to realize that when she was overwhelmed with work or felt pressure in other areas of her life, she didn't turn to Robert. In fact, she preferred not to see him at all during those times. She withdrew from the support she believed would not be there.

Reciprocally, Robert expressed his greatest concern: "Will I ever be enough for Diane?" His question spoke volumes about the separateness of their lives. Both Diane's withholding and Robert's fear kept them from becoming united as a dating couple, and promised to seriously damage their prospective marriage.

Think of your most recent physical union with your spouse. Was it symbolic of the present union of your lives and hearts? Did it represent the way you *feel* about each other? If you withhold your heart, if you keep your hopes and dreams to yourself because you fear they will be ridiculed, it will show in your sexual relationship. Everything you hold back from your spouse affects your marital intimacy, which is why lies of any kind are so difficult to keep hidden. They manifest themselves in marital union—or non-union. Every lie (white, gray, or black) diminishes spouses' capacity to experience marital intimacy. Hearts and minds cannot be one when one spouse is working to conceal and the other is working to reveal.

What does being one with your spouse mean to you? One woman said, "Peace settles on my heart when I think of being one with my husband. It is a peace that surpasses understanding and explanation. I may not know how to describe it, but I know the feeling. When I see my husband diligently and joyfully trying to do whatever the Lord has asked him to do, being one with my husband—in every way—is where I most want to be, any day, anytime."

How do you and your spouse unite in ways other than physical union? What needs to change in your relationship so that other areas of your lives are joined together? Do you talk with each other, work on problems together, enjoy small moments together, and savor the joy of just being together? Can you laugh *together* rather than at one another? One woman realized that pure laughter united her heart with her husband's. In fact, she said, "I've learned that while anger kills my desire for physical intimacy, laughter gives life to it."

How united are you and your spouse in such daily activities as teaching your children and paying your bills? How united are your thoughts and feelings? Do you share activities, thoughts, and feelings with each other on a regular basis? Or at present, do you share little more than pressure, conflict, and disagreement? The more you learn and work to share everything, the less frequently will negative emotions erupt between you and the more united you will be.

UNITY BECOMES YOU

Some may fear, "But won't I lose my identity if I focus on being one with my spouse?" Actually, in a marriage where there is unity of feeling and unity of purpose, each spouse becomes even more of who he or she really is. Union of feeling creates an environment where spouses' spirits can grow, develop, and shine. In a marriage where marital intimacy becomes a symbol of their emotional and spiritual unity, over time spouses become more and more like their true selves. One woman, now well into her eighties and married for six decades, said of her husband, "He has always let me be myself. He has always let me soar." In toxic and troubled relationships, on the other hand, spouses' spirits become wounded and shrunken, territoriality is a problem, both are filled with fear, and spouses become rigid fragments of themselves.

Again the Savior's teachings help us: "Take my yoke upon you, and learn of me . . . ," He says, "For my yoke is easy, and my burden is light." (Matthew 11:29–30.) As in all things, the Lord is the ultimate example. Just as He invites us to yoke ourselves to Him, for therein lies the greatest strength, couples who work to become more fully and equally yoked together will feel their burdens being lightened. And one of the most important things spouses can learn through this yoking process is how much they really love each other and want to pull together.

UNITED WE STAND

Imagine how different your life would be if you felt that every problem "you" had was a problem for you *and* your spouse—that every success was a success for both of you.

A husband was finally able to conquer pornography's demoralizing rule over his life when he began to trust that he and his wife were working together as a team in the war against the adversary's control of his mind and heart. With great anguish and relief he confessed to his wife, "I've been having a terrible time at work. I've been looking at things on the Internet that are wrong—in fact, they're evil. I've even skipped out of work a few times in the afternoon to go see erotic movies. And I've been getting up at night when you're asleep and going into my den and visiting pornographic web sites. I'm so ashamed. I feel so helpless. I'm disgusted with myself, and I'm embarrassed to tell you this because I thought I was making progress. I thought I could just hide this relapse and deal with it myself."

His wife rose to the occasion and commended him for his strength in speaking up. She assured him that since he never really experienced pornography by himself—that is, he always brought its influence back to their marriage—he didn't have to manage the problem by himself. It was *their* problem, not *his* problem. She would join him in fighting the problem. Together they would cast pornography out of their lives rather than casting each other out. They started to work on their "team strategies." One of the things they decided was that he would call her from work if he was tempted to view something pornographic. He would run to "them," to the strength of their unity.

As this couple came to experience that marital intimacy is truly a symbol of unity, they were mobilized and empowered to withstand the temptations of the adversary *together.* Through their union of feelings of love, courage, and hope, they gained power—even power with God—to dissipate the husband's despair and immobilizing guilt, and the wife's past recriminating words and behaviors, all of which had previously perpetuated *their* pornography problem.

Another couple, married only a few months, were struggling with "sexual compatibility." When they started to think about the problem as "our marital intimacy problem," rather than as "her frigidity problem" or "his impulse control problem," they started to find solutions. As the wife said, "When I think of the situation as 'our' problem, I'm energized to work with my husband to solve it. It feels like we're a team over here and the problem is over there. It's 'us' against 'it,' and 'it' seems so much smaller than before. I feel hopeful, rather than guilty and frustrated, and so much more united with my husband."

Such unity is enhanced by uniting with the Lord and seeking His help together. Strength to stand together really comes when spouses kneel together in prayer. President Hinckley has counseled: "Believe in prayer. There is nothing like it. When all is said and done there is no power on earth like the power of prayer." (*Church News*, January 29, 2000, 5.) There is no power like that which comes by kneeling with your spouse and seeking the Lord's help to become more united, to be more effective as a team tackling all of the "our" difficulties, concerns, and problems that have constrained your marital intimacy.

SYMBOLS: MESSAGES AND MEANINGS

Husbands and wives send a multitude of messages through their words and their behavior, and their spouses interpret such words and actions as measures of devotion and commitment. One afternoon a young husband, an avid golfer, played eighteen holes with friends, returning home forty-five minutes late for a trip with his wife to his sister-in-law's birthday party. His wife (and their car) were no longer waiting for him. However, what was waiting was a card and a beautifully wrapped box with his name on it. Inside the box was a new golf ball. Inside the card was his wife's sentiment that the real treasure in his life was clearly golf, not her feelings or their marriage. He promptly hitchhiked to his wife's sister's home, forty miles away, and apologized to his wife. Further, he promised never to put golf ahead of her again. And he backed up his words by being true to his promise. In time, his wife began to believe him—because she experienced day by day that his commitment was indeed to their marriage.

This husband's commitment led him and his wife to discover the truth that when spouses unite their lives in every way, marital intimacy becomes a symbol that keeps on giving. It offers more strength, unity, joy, power, healing, light, and love than either spouse could ever find on his or her own or with anyone else.

This couple also learned that when spouses are united, their desire for marital intimacy naturally follows. There is no forcing or withholding, no headaches or power struggles, no silent treatments or jammed time schedules that can prevent their intimate times together.

PHYSICAL INTIMACY: A SACRED SYMBOL

Joseph Fielding McConkie has said, "Symbols are the language of the scriptures, the language of revelation, the language of the Spirit, the language of faith. . . . Symbols are the language in which all gospel covenants and ordinances of salvation have been revealed. They are the means whereby we enrich, deepen and enhance understanding and expression." (*Gospel Symbolism*, 1.)

All things were created by the Savior. As John the Beloved wrote, "All things were made by him; and without him was not any thing made that was made." (John 1:3.) Thus, all things are made to bear record of the Savior. (See Moses 6:63.) Our very creation and our bodies, which have the ability to procreate, bear record of Him.

Referring to physical intimacy, Elder Jeffrey R. Holland has said, "Physiologically we are created as men and women to fit together in such a union." ("Of Souls, Symbols, and Sacraments," 159.) Some people ask, "Why? Why that way? Why not another way to unite physically?" But the union that occurs in marital intimacy is a perfect symbol—a symbol from which we can learn a great deal.

The sacred areas of our bodies that unite in physical intimacy are physiologically prepared to respond in a way that co-creates love. Surely, our physiological responses are intended to be more than Pavlovian conditioned responses. Physiological arousal of sacred body parts can be triggered by anything from the mention of a name to a strain of music to the sight of something. So, too, physiological arousal can be restrained through adverse pairing with pain, disdain, humiliation, or abuse. Sadly, much marital intimacy can be held captive because of the past experiences of one or both spouses. If spouses have had experiences that have distorted their natural passions, they may sometimes seek unnatural methods of "fulfillment" that can never satisfy (such as masturbation) or turn away altogether (frigidity and impotence) from the fulfillment true marital intimacy can bring.

Since marital intimacy is to be a symbol, what kind of symbol is it? It is "a symbol that demands special sanctity," explained Elder Jeffrey R. Holland. ("Of Souls, Symbols, and Sacraments," 156.) Without unity of lives, without the sanctity of the symbol, spouses focus on the physical act only—and on the physical act as nothing more than physical. But such an approach would be akin to kneeling on a wrestling mat in a gymnasium as contrasted with kneeling at an altar in the temple. One is nothing but a physical act. The other is a sublimely sacred symbol.

So what are we to understand about life and love, about merging and marriage, through the symbol of marital intimacy? As one righteous and articulate wife, mother, and grandmother considered the symbol of marital intimacy, she said: "I believe that physical union is a completion of the temple sealing. It is the completion of the temple covenants—truly consummating the love that brought you to the temple. Physical love is like a seal upon a seal."

What do we understand about symbols that can help us as we seek further truth about the grand symbol of marital intimacy? Perhaps as we seek to understand this symbol in the same way that we seek deeper meaning in other sacred symbols, we will be taught. As we wrap our minds and hearts around the Lord's use of symbolism, we could ask ourselves (and the Lord) such questions as:

• What does that symbol mean to me now?

• What message is the Lord trying to give me through that symbol?

• Do I understand the symbol the way I should?

• Do I feel about the symbol the way I should?

Now, what might happen as we ask ourselves these same questions about the symbol of marital intimacy?

• What does the symbol of marital intimacy mean to me these days?

• What message and understanding is the Lord trying to give me through the symbol of marital intimacy?

• Do I understand the symbol of marital intimacy the way I should?

• Do I feel about the symbol of marital intimacy the way I should?

As we are obedient to what the Lord has already taught us about His symbols, He will teach us more. There is a direct connection between our worthiness, our humility, and our pleadings with the Lord and the increase in our understanding of this life-generating and love-sustaining symbol, physical intimacy.

QUESTIONS TO CONSIDER

• What comes to your mind when you think about marital intimacy as a symbol of how united you and your spouse really are?

• If you wanted to show your increasing commitment to your spouse—your desire to be more united in everything, in every way—how could you show it this very day?

• Are there opportunities to join your life with that of your spouse that you may have been overlooking?

Chapter 11

SACRED INTIMACY
CAN BE SANCTIFYING

True marital intimacy can be sacred and sanctifying, a time to draw closer to God. It can be a time "when we quite literally unite our will with God's will, our spirit with His spirit, where communion through the veil becomes very real." (Jeffrey R. Holland, *Ensign,* November 1998, 77.) What a profound truth that, sadly, is the exact opposite of what many men and women believe. Influenced by the "traditions of their fathers and mothers," many husbands and wives have supposed that they were never further away from the Lord than when joining together in physical union. Nothing could be further from the truth!

So now let's think about the real truth: "Sexual union is . . . , in its own profound way, a genuine sacrament of the highest order, a union not only of a man and a woman but also very much the union of that man and woman with God." (Holland, "Of Souls, Symbols, and Sacraments," 163.) If it seems like a giant leap to even consider the truth of marital intimacy as a kind of sacramental experience, would you be willing to believe that it is indeed a *quantum* leap—a leap forward into truth!

It is difficult for many to think about physical intimacy as a kind of sacred privilege. "Do you mean that sex is supposed to be a spiritual experience?" one woman said in amazement. And a husband retorted, "You've got to be kidding! I never feel less spiritual than when I'm preparing for, or engaging in, sexual experiences! Spiritual feelings are for church. Spiritual things and sex are two really different things to me. It almost seems sacrilegious to think about sex as a time to draw close to God!"

For a moment, let's suspend those objections and try to think about physical intimacy as a kind of sacramental moment. What might that possibly mean? Think about sacramental moments, moments when "we not only acknowledge [God's] divinity but we quite literally take something of that divinity to ourselves. . . . Those special moments include kneeling at a marriage altar in the house of the Lord, blessing a newborn baby, baptizing and confirming a new member of the Church, [and] partaking of the emblems of the Lord's Supper." (Holland, *Ensign*, November 1998, 77.)

Have you ever considered that marital intimacy might have something in common with baptism, confirmation, temple sealings, baby blessings, and even the Sacrament? Such a perspective helps us begin to understand the exquisite sacredness of physical intimacy and the profound significance and influence of co-creating love in marriage! However, *begin to understand* is the operative phrase. As one faithful wife of great spiritual depth and understanding expressed it: "I believe marital intimacy can be a kind of sacramental moment, and that this is the ideal. This is a very spiritually mature concept that a couple works toward. It should not cause spouses to be critical of each other if their experience does not yet achieve this ideal. It might be like expecting a child to understand the Atonement when she is just being introduced to the bread and water of the Sacrament."

A Kind of Sacrament

If we are to envision physical intimacy as a kind of sacrament, it seems appropriate to consider what happens during the Sacrament. "The Sacramental prayers invite personal introspection, repentance, and rededication, yet they are also communal, binding individuals into congregations who jointly and publicly attest to their willingness to remember Christ. This shared commitment to become like Christ, repeated weekly, defines the supreme aspiration of Latter-day Saint life." (*Scriptures of the Church*, 563.)

The Sacrament prayers focus our minds and hearts on the Savior, on all that He has done for us, and on what we can do to draw closer to Him. Healing occurs. "You feel the wounds of the spirit being healed, and the load being lifted," said Elder Melvin J. Ballard. (Hinckley, *Sermons and Missionary Services of Melvin J. Ballard*, 148–49.) The portals of heaven open. The Holy Ghost attends us. As we remember the Savior and keep His commandments, we can have the palpable experience Jacob describes of having the Lord pour His Spirit into our souls. (See Jacob 7:8.) As we partake worthily of the Sacrament, we indeed take part of divinity to ourselves and thus become a little more godlike. And as Elder Tad R. Callister explained, "as we become more godlike we become more powerful. Knowledge brings power; purity brings power; love brings power." (*The Infinite Atonement*, 68.)

Would thinking about these truths in a parallel fashion in relation to marital intimacy expand our ability to understand it as a sacred experience? From time to time, worthily partaking of marital intimacy can similarly involve "personal introspection, repentance, and rededication." It can bind spouses closer in their commitment to each other and to the Lord. Physical intimacy can be a time when healing occurs, when "the wounds of the spirit [are] healed, and the load [is] lifted," when the portals of heaven open, when the Holy Ghost attends a husband and wife *together* in a profound way. It can be a time when spouses could use Jacob's words to describe their experience: "The Lord God poured in his Spirit into my soul." (Jacob 7:8.) As spouses partake worthily of these sacred marital privileges, they can indeed take part of divinity to themselves and become a bit more godlike and more powerful.

POTENTIAL POWER

What is the power available to spouses through marital intimacy? Can our minds and hearts even conceive of the power that is there? What do we really comprehend about the power to procreate, about the amazing power to join with God in preparing a body for one of His spirit children?

Access to the power to procreate requires a husband and wife to be joined physically together. It is impossible to procreate alone or with someone of one's own gender. Rightly used, the power to procreate is an exclusive power, reserved for husbands and wives.

Tragically, the God-given power of procreation is frequently neither honored nor used wisely. It is often abused. But when it is honored, other powers await. Husbands and wives have reported that powers connected to marital intimacy include:

• the power to love (even those who don't "deserve" it).

• the power to feel loved (even if you have never experienced love before).

• the power to feel worthy of love (even if you've doubted your worth all your life).

• the power to heal (even wounds that you did not cause and that have festered for years).

• the power to be healed (even though you may have doubted your worthiness to be healed).

• the power to repent (even though it is painful).

• the power to forgive (even those who don't repent, or those who have repeatedly hurt you).

• the power to remember your true identity as a son or daughter of God (even though sometimes you forget).

• the power to remember premortal assignments (even though you feel inadequate in your day-to-day activities).

• the power to see each other as the Savior does (even though the years may have blinded you to each other's good intents and great hearts).

These powers are available to spouses through marital intimacy that is undergirded by the personal purity of each spouse. Personal purity brings forth pure love, the kind Parley P. Pratt described when he said:

"I had loved before, but I knew not why. But now I loved—with a pureness—an intensity of elevated, exalted feeling, which would lift my soul from the transitory things of this groveling sphere and expand it as the ocean.

"I felt that God was Heavenly Father indeed; that Jesus was my brother, and that the wife of my bosom was an immortal, eternal companion. . . .

"In short, I could now love with the spirit and with the understanding also." (*Autobiography of Parley P. Pratt*, 297, 298.)

Just as there is a wonderful, palpable reciprocity between personal purity and partaking of the Sacrament, there is a reciprocity between unity and physical intimacy, and another between personal purity and physical love. Consider the marvelous virtuous cycles that can bless husbands' and wives' lives. We come to the Sacrament table with hearts as pure and hands as clean as possible. Then, through partaking of the Sacrament, we become more clean and more pure because of the power of the Atonement. Likewise, while spouses need to be united in their lives and hearts and minds to experience true marital intimacy, marital intimacy also creates more unity. And while marital intimacy is to be partaken of worthily, physical intimacy can also increase the purity of the spouses. As President Joseph F. Smith taught, "Sexual union . . . if participated in with right intent is honorable and sanctifying." (*Gospel Doctrine*, 309.) What hopeful and merciful and encouraging truths!

Marital intimacy can be sanctifying, life-giving, and love-generating. It can indeed be a kind of sacrament when it involves the uniting of a husband's body and spirit with his wife's body and spirit, when it springs from complete unity of their lives, and when it involves the Spirit and brings the couple closer to the Savior.

An Act of Love Ordained by God

Marital intimacy is an act of love, ordained by God, that offers access to His power in order to co-create life and love. Sadly, far too many couples live far beneath their privileges because they look to the world for their standards of sexually appropriate behavior. The chasm seems to grow wider by the day between eternal truths about marital intimacy and the world's views—which are polluted with Lucifer's lies. (See Appendix.)

When we really believe that there is a kind of power and love and an experience of intimacy that goes beyond anything the most "romantic" movie portrays, then settling for what Hollywood promises rather than embracing what holy prophets have taught is worse than a sham, it's a shame.

President Boyd K. Packer anticipated attacks on marital intimacy that even come from within marriage. He admonished, "[You] may be tempted to introduce things into your relationship which are unworthy. Do not, as the scriptures warn, 'change the natural use into that which is against nature' (Romans 1:26). If you do, the tempter will drive a wedge between you." (*The Things of the Soul*, 113.) Anything that offends the Spirit or either spouse's spirit will allow the tempter to drive a wedge between husbands and wives.

"I was talked out of my feelings"—such are the haunting words of a woman whose husband on their wedding night introduced her to the consummation of their love in a manner that offended her spirit. For years they carried on the mirage of a marriage and the illusion of intimacy. That was the best they could do, this woman who felt numb and this man who felt rejected.

Life is filled with unexpected events. But if we are prepared we shall not fear! Perhaps spouses need to be prepared to respond to illicit requests from their companions with something such as: "This doesn't seem or feel right to me."

A dramatic change in the quality of their marital union occurred for one couple when the husband reminded himself prior to each intimate experience, "Our marital intimacy can be a sacred time—a time to reunite with my wife and to feel the Spirit. It is a time to remember all that my wife has done for me, and to remember and celebrate the love she has for me and the love I have for her." This husband's formerly disappointing and often distressing sexual invitations to his wife were replaced with invitations that honored his wife and their sacred intimate moments.

Latter-day Saints who have made sacred covenants with the Lord will never be truly happy participating in sinful sexual practices. They may periodically and erroneously believe they are finding happiness in sinful sex, but to be truly fulfilling, the Spirit needs to sanction the intimate experience.

A Time to Remember, Review, and Renew

There is power in remembering, reviewing, and renewing. What strength might come to a couple as they remember their temple covenants, even repeating in their minds the words of their temple sealing? During a difficult period in one couple's marriage, they frequently returned to the temple to participate in proxy sealings so they could remember and review the covenants they had made during their own temple wedding. As they repeated in their minds the words of their temple sealing, their love was expanded, purified, and solidified. Over time, they discovered that for them their physically intimate moments prompted a most natural and wonderful review of their covenants of marriage with the Lord and with each other.

During the Sacrament we review our past week and the need for repentance in our lives. Marital intimacy can also prompt such a review. One wife found that as her heart was drawn out to her husband while they were co-creating love, her mind was also drawn to reflect on the past week. She found that it was the perfect time to make new resolves to do better and be kinder to her husband—a time to repent of her unkind or thoughtless words and actions.

Marital intimacy can prompt us to remember our true identity as children of heavenly parents, as men and women of God. It can reassure us that we are worthy of love. A woman spoke of times when her husband, ravaged by self-doubts and collisions with the brutal world, felt unworthy in almost every way. She then said tenderly—almost reverently—"In those moments, physical intimacy was the only way I could help him feel loved—worthy of love   worthy to love." Think of the power of this sacred uniting! Think of the healing power—the sealing power!

One husband spoke of how remembering the Savior blessed his intimacy with his wife: "Sometimes our sexual uniting feels so sacred that it really does feel like a kind of sacrament. After these unique times I find it easier to think about the Savior. I feel closer to Him and to my wife during these times than at any other time." He further described the feelings of love and joy that supported their marriage of more than forty years: "Sometimes it feels as though the Lord has been blessing our sacred, intimate time together and that we are the only ones in the world."

Notice this man's use of the word *sometimes*. Even couples who have grown strong in their understanding of this sacred principle acknowledge that powerful spiritual stirrings do not always accompany their time together. Does that mean they have failed, or somehow been less worthy? Certainly not. As the old saying suggests, "Ideals are stars to steer by, not sticks to beat ourselves with."

One woman likened her feelings about intimacy to what she experienced attending the temple. "Sometimes when I go to the temple it seems like I receive all kinds of inspiration. Thoughts fill my mind, and my understanding takes a leap. Other times, I'm happy to be there, but it's more an exercise in obedience. I feel good, but not as inspired. I assume these peaks and plateaus in my temple experience are a reflection of my own spiritual growth curve."

The same principle applies to marital intimacy. Worthily partaken of, sexual intimacy is always a blessing, but the emotions and feelings involved may vary. The goal is to be steadily and gradually progressing in what this sacred intimacy is bringing you, your spouse, and your marriage.

OTHER EFFECTS OF REMEMBERING

As spouses begin to accept the grand truth that marital intimacy can be sacramental in nature, what happens?

One husband dramatically quickened his reaction time in his efforts to avoid sexually explicit information on the Internet because of this truth. He reminded himself, "If I choose to look at these images that are so damaging to my spirit and so offending to the Spirit, I am really choosing to have a less satisfying intimate experience with my wife. I will be choosing to be unable to take part of deity into myself when my wife and I join together in what can be a sacred moment."

Conduct and conversations change in the presence of truth. A wife and mother found that when she started to think of the potential sacramental nature of marital intimacy, her former feelings of embarrassment in teaching her children about intimacy fell away. Instead, she felt an increased love and gratitude for her husband and the Savior, and she began to find natural opportunities to fulfill her teaching privileges as a mother.

A wife pled in prayer to know how to support her husband

following his disfellowshipment. The following words came to her mind: "We can be more like the Savior by healing wounds we did not cause." Realizing how much her husband needed experiences with the Spirit and with the sacred, and understanding that marital intimacy can be a kind of sacrament, she offered her love to him in this sacred way without hesitation or qualification. And all were blessed. In seeking to heal her husband, she herself was healed, receiving more light and love. Her own pain, which had been caused by the sins of her husband, was lessened, and her love for her husband and the Lord grew.

A young wife was experiencing difficulties with the transition from keeping the law of chastity as a single woman to keeping the law of chastity within the bounds and bonds of marriage. After living a sexually pure life before she was married, she struggled with participating in physical intimacy with her husband. She felt like a failure in her marriage of only six months. In her mind she knew that sexual union was "more than okay" for spouses and that in fact it was commended and commanded by the Lord. But her feelings remained "frozen." "I just don't know what to do," she grieved. "I want to show love to my husband in this way, and I know that I should, but I can still hear my Young Women leaders counseling against it in my mind."

A turning point came for this wife when she started to think about physical intimacy as a kind of sacramental moment. The truth set her feelings free. She was almost euphoric when she said, "When I remember that sexual intimacy with my husband can be a sacred time for us to draw closer to each other and to the Lord—well, that makes all the difference!"

The Lord blesses those who love according to His pattern— spouses who love each other purely and who partake of marital intimacy with pure intent. (See Joseph F. Smith, *Gospel Doctrine*, 309.) He loves spouses whose passions and appetites have been purified, intensified, and magnified by the Holy Ghost.

A QUESTION TO CONSIDER

As you and your spouse consider that one of the primary purposes of the marital intimacy is to bring you as a couple closer to the Lord than you have ever been before, how does that influence your activities before, during, and after co-creating love?

PART 5

WHAT DO
WE DO NOW?

*It is one thing to talk about the importance and
sanctity of marriage, and another thing entirely to create
such a marriage, day in and day out. Marriage can be fragile.
It requires nurture and time and very much effort.*
—Gordon B. Hinckley,
Standing for Something, 127

Chapter 12

PREPARING
FOR INTIMACY

The Lord's counsel in the 88th section of the Doctrine and Covenants is a wonderful guide for spouses: "Cease from all your light speeches . . . from all your lustful desires, from all your pride and light-mindedness, and from all your wicked doings. . . . See that ye love one another; cease to be covetous; learn to impart one to another. . . . Cease to be idle; cease to be unclean; cease to find fault one with another; cease to sleep longer than is needful; retire to thy bed early, that ye may not be weary; arise early, that your bodies and your minds may be invigorated. And above all things, clothe yourselves with the bond of charity." (D&C 88:121, 123–25.) This advice could form the foundation of an entire marriage manual!

In fact, many problems that plague marriages would be eliminated if these words of the Lord were obeyed. The following table suggests a few ways they might be applied:

Marital Problem	The Lord's Solution
Criticism and emotional abuse	Cease to find fault; cease from all pride
Hygiene/housekeeping problems	Cease to be unclean
Pornography	Cease your lustful desires and wicked doings; cease to be unclean
Adultery	Cease to be covetous; cease your lustful desires and wicked doings; cease to be unclean
Trivializing marital intimacy itself	Cease from all your light speeches and light-mindedness
Selfishness	Learn to impart one to another
Pride	Cease from all your pride
Financial problems	Cease to be idle; cease to be covetous; cease from all your pride
Communication problems	Cease to find fault; cease from your pride; learn to impart one to another; cease from all your light speeches
Laziness; "underinvolvement" in caring for the home and family	Cease to be idle; cease to sleep longer than is needful; retire to bed early and arise early that your bodies and minds may be invigorated

Now, consider what would happen if the Lord's instructions of *what to do* in the midst of all that "ceasing" were followed: "See that ye love one another. . . . And above all things, clothe yourselves with the bond of charity." Imagine how well prepared for marital intimacy husbands and wives would be if just that one injunction were really followed!

LET THE HOLY SPIRIT GUIDE

As men and women of Christ and of covenant, we can never expect to find a fulness of joy by following the world's prescription for sexual intimacy. We can't participate in "all that is in the world, the lust of the flesh, and the lust of the eyes, and the pride of life" and still do "the will of God." (1 John 2:16–17.) Paul's words provide a great guideline for spouses seeking to prepare for co-creating love. He counsels, "Refuse profane and old wives' fables, and exercise thyself rather unto godliness." (1 Timothy 4:7.) Looking beyond the world's "profane and old wives' fables" can help Latter-day Saint couples prepare for God-ordained sexual intimacy.

One bewildered husband said, "Okay, now I know what I'm *not* supposed to do. But I don't have a clue about what I *should* do. I want to be able to offer my wife the kind of marital intimacy we're talking about, but if I can't take my lead from what I see on TV and in movies, what do I do? I'm not good at thinking of these things myself."

Fortunately, this husband doesn't have to figure out by himself how to prepare for marital intimacy, and neither do you. Consider some of the spiritual truths we have discussed. We start with the foundational understanding that intimacy of any kind involves reciprocal feelings of trust and emotional closeness and an open communication of thoughts and feelings. Hence, the more a husband and wife experience open communication, trust, and emotional closeness with each other, the greater their prospects for enjoying true marital intimacy. The more unified spouses are in all areas of their lives, the more intimate their relationship will be. Physical intimacy then becomes a symbol of their overall unity. True marital intimacy becomes a time for them to draw closer to each other by uniting their whole souls—bodies and spirits. And it becomes a time when spouses can draw closer to the Lord. With these ideas in mind, it follows naturally then that any activity that (1) draws spouses' hearts out to one another and (2) invites the Spirit will help prepare a couple for marital intimacy.

The more you prepare yourself spiritually, bringing yourself more in tune with your spouse's spirit and with the Spirit, the more fulfilling your sexual experiences will become over time. In the words of one wife, "I never feel closer to my husband than when he is under the influence of the Spirit." Another wife said, "The greatest elixir of love for me is when my husband says, 'I want to spend time with you,' 'I want to know what's really on your mind,' 'How are you really doing?'" As spouses seek the Lord's help about how to prepare for marital intimacy, the Holy Ghost will whisper truth-filled directives especially for them.

Thirty Activities That Can Increase Feelings of Intimacy

Following are thirty activities that various couples have found draw their hearts out to one another and invite the Spirit, setting the stage for greater intimacy in their relationship.

1. Think and ask about how your spouse is really doing and feeling.

2. Do things to lift your spouse's burdens and to let your spouse know that he or she is not alone. In other words, shore up your spouse's feeble knees and strengthen his or her hands that hang down.

3. Think about what would help strengthen your spouse's spirit and help him or her feel better about himself or herself.

4. Do things together—walk, work, play, dream, spend, and save *together*.

5. Talk and express your thoughts and feelings before, during, and after physically intimate moments.

6. Be involved in each other's lives and in the lives of your children. (As one woman said, "When I see my husband involved with our children, my heart is irresistibly drawn out to him.")

7. Draw a boundary around your marital intimacy. Keep the in-laws and your children and friends out. This is your sacred space and private experience. Keep it as yours alone.

8. Create a private sanctuary for the two of you—and include a lock on the door.

9. Take responsibility for what you do to contribute to the problems in your marriage. Apologize sincerely. Ask for forgiveness and willingly offer forgiveness.

10. Pray together and individually to hear the voice of the Lord.

11. Look for subtle—and not-so-subtle—ways that the adversary is holding your marriage hostage. Talk with each other about it.

12. Cast Satan out of your lives and your relationship.

13. Seek ideas for strengthening your marriage in the scriptures, together and individually.

14. Use "we," "us," and "our" language in public and in private.

15. Designate one time a week that is just for the two of you to talk and be together.

16. Go to the temple together, remember your covenants, and talk about how you felt there, what came to your mind, what you learned.

17. Fast together for your marriage.

18. Look into your spouse's eyes—really look.

19. Smile and laugh together.

20. Comment on your spouse's strengths, both privately and publicly.

21. Turn to each other first when there are challenges. Cry together when the occasion warrants it.

22. Thank your spouse.

23. Thank the Lord for your spouse.

24. Express love for your spouse in word and deed—more than he or she would ever expect—in private and in public.

25. Express love for the Lord privately and publicly—frequently.

26. Remember that you are a child of God with divine characteristics and potential.

27. Remember that you've made sacred covenants with your spouse and with the Lord.

28. Remember that true marital intimacy involves the uniting of your souls—your body and spirit joining with the body and spirit of your spouse.

29. Remember that co-creating love is to be symbolic of the total unity that can exist between you and your spouse.

30. Remember that marital intimacy can be a kind of sacrament. It can be a time to draw closer to the Lord together and receive of His power.

This list is neither prescriptive nor all-inclusive. Not all of these activities that have helped other couples prepare for marital intimacy may fit for you. Co-creating love is unique for each couple. As you and your spouse seek and ask, you will find the appropriate activities that will help you lay claim to, or perhaps reclaim, the marital intimacy that is yours to enjoy.

With the understanding that each couple needs to be led by the Spirit to discover how to feel closer to each other, perhaps the following general guidelines can provide some initial assistance for your adventure.

BURY YOUR WEAPONS OF WAR

In the days of Ammon in the Book of Mormon, the converted Lamanites were worried about staining their swords with the blood of their enemies. They wanted war to end. So, "they buried their weapons of war, for peace." (Alma 24:19.) What a dramatic gesture to signify just how determined they were to have peace!

Most husbands and wives can identify the weapons of war that fight against their marital intimacy. These weapons of war are thoughts, feelings, and behaviors that keep spouses feeling separate and single within their marriages. These weapons wound, maim, destroy, defile, or kill marital intimacy. As long as spouses continue to wield these weapons of war, the possibility of achieving true marital intimacy is out of the question.

One couple took the above scripture in Alma to heart. They made lists of words, thoughts, feelings, and behaviors that killed their desire for marital intimacy. For example, the husband said, "I never want to say to you again: 'You control me when you disapprove of what I'm watching on TV.' I want to bury that weapon. The truth is that what you think about me really matters to me and helps me. Stubborn pride has prevented me from listening to your fears. From now on I won't fight you anymore about TV viewing that makes you feel uncomfortable. I also want to bury the belief that 'I will never be good enough for you.' You've shown me and told me otherwise over and over again. I want to lay down that weapon of war and bury it."

He kept adding to his list of things he used as "weapons of war" against his wife, himself, and their relationship. He also listed words, thoughts, feelings, and behaviors that he felt were "weapons of war" used by his wife. His wife did the same. As they reviewed their lists, they found some weapons that they needed each other's help to overcome. They talked about those things and what still needed to change before they would be able to bury those weapons. For example, one weapon could not be buried until an apology was offered and accepted.

The process took several weeks of intensively detecting old weapons, talking, and writing. Once the lists were made, they then wrote each "weapon of war" on a separate piece of paper. Ceremonially placing each piece of paper in a box, they vowed to each other to never again use that weapon. So committed were they to ridding their relationship of these destructive words, thoughts, and practices that they then selected a safe and private place to bury the box, declaring that if they ever were tempted to use any of those weapons again, they would need to go to the burial site together, dig up the box, and exhume the remains to find the weapon they wanted to use. And thus they "buried their weapons of war deep in the earth, because of their love towards their [spouse]." (Alma 26:32.)

BRING BROKEN HEARTS
AND CONTRITE SPIRITS

In D&C 59:8 we read about how to prepare ourselves to partake of the Sacrament of the Lord's Supper: We are each to bring a broken (or open) heart and a contrite spirit. What a great guideline for spouses as they prepare for sacred marital intimacy!

One couple's preparation included a heart-to-heart conversation where they laid their pride aside, expressed sorrow for past offenses, and resolved to be more loving and more pure. They also determined to live by the "48-hour rule" to manage future disappointments. If one of them was upset about something the other did or didn't do, he or she had 48 hours following the "offense" to talk with the offender about it. If they didn't bring up what was troubling them within 48 hours, it was not fair to bring it up after that time period. This rule helped them stop their destructive former practice of reciting each other's past sins, mistakes, and omissions whenever one of them did anything wrong. This couple's pattern of flogging each other with the past decreased, and they started building a future together—one that began to include moments of true marital intimacy.

As the couple continued to uncover the effects of pride in their marriage the wife said, "I think I've missed many opportunities to help you learn to love. I was given lots of love growing up and saw a great example in my parents of a husband and wife who really enjoyed each other and supported each other in every way. I thought the other day that if you had a bandage over your heart with a sign on it that said, 'In need of learning about love,' I would be much more gentle and giving and forgiving of you. I'm sorry that I've punished you for not knowing how to love me."

FOCUS ON LOVE-GENERATING IMAGES

One couple earnestly sought to put behind them the world's approach to "making love." They longed to gain access to the binding power that could come from worthily co-creating love. One day in prayer the wife was blessed with powerful, positive images of her husband. These images came into her mind and stayed in her heart. In her prayerful, seeking state, she was given to understand that these were sacred images of her husband's premortal self. As she mentally embraced these images, her heart was irresistibly drawn out to her husband in a manner unlike anything she had previously experienced. And each time the wife brought these images to her mind, she experienced a heightened appreciation for her husband and a desire to unite her life with his in every way.

REMEMBER YOUR COVENANTS

Christian writer C. S. Lewis offers us an important truth in the form of advice from Screwtape, a senior devil, writing to his apprenticing nephew, Wormwood: "It is funny how mortals always picture us as putting things into their minds: in reality our best work is done by keeping things out." (*Screwtape Letters,* 25.)

What have you forgotten lately about the Savior, yourself, your spouse, your relationship, or about love and marriage that may be adversely affecting your marital intimacy?

How would remembering your temple wedding ceremony help you enjoy physical intimacy even more? Temple weddings involve symbols, not the least of which is the symbol of leaving the world in order to enter the temple. Through keeping the Lord's commandments, you came out of the world, both literally and symbolically, to participate in your temple wedding. You shut the world out so that you and your beloved could be joined together in an endless contract—sealed together.

Elder John A. Widtsoe spoke of the elegant orchestration of a temple wedding and the benefits of really concentrating on the true meaning of the ceremony: "[Temple weddings] are performed in an attractive sealing room, especially dedicated for the purpose. The ceremony itself is simple, beautiful, and profound. Relatively few witnesses are present. Quiet and order prevail. There are no external trappings to confuse the mind. Full attention may be given to the sacred covenants to be made, and the blessings to follow cover the vast period of eternal existence." (*Evidences and Reconciliations*, 232.)

Are you keeping the door to the world closed behind you as a couple, as you are in the process of building upon your temple wedding ceremony to fashion your temple marriage? If you consider the temple wedding ceremony to be a pattern for happiness within your marital intimacy:

• Do you give your full attention to your spouse from time to time?

• Do quiet and order prevail during moments of marital intimacy?

• Is your marriage free from excessive external trappings?

• Do you regularly review your sacred covenants and the associated blessings?

PRAY FOR GIFTS OF THE SPIRIT

Tad R. Callister has written, "President George Q. Cannon . . . eloquently and fervently pleaded with the saints to overcome each manifested weakness through the acquisition of a countermanding gift of strength, known as a gift of the Spirit." (*The*

Infinite Atonement, 273.) What gifts of the Spirit would strengthen you and your spouse? Talk about this with your spouse. Determine to seek and pray for those gifts of the Spirit that would increase the feelings of intimacy in your marriage. (See D&C 46 and Moroni 10 for a beginning listing of possible gifts of the Spirit.)

For one couple, the seemingly simple act of reading about gifts of the Spirit was a major turning point in their marriage. Following a difficult time, the husband resolved not to approach his wife sexually until he felt "more worthy." In the midst of this self-imposed restraint, he read to his wife one evening from section 46 of the Doctrine and Covenants. Her heart was irresistibly drawn toward his. She later described that experience as the most wonderful time—in twenty-five years of marriage—of uniting their spirits, an important prerequisite to uniting their whole souls in marital intimacy.

LISTEN TO MUSIC THAT BRINGS YOUR SPIRIT TO LIFE

Listening to music can lift us and rescue us from the darkness of the world. One couple loved music. Playing "their song" and listening to "mood music" was a favorite part of their preparation for physical intimacy. The melodies, words, rhythms, and volumes varied from selection to selection, but the outcome was always the same: Each piece of music brought their spirits to life.

SPEAK WORDS OF LOVE AND COMMITMENT

As stated earlier, the "first four minutes of contact" between a couple are important in drawing their hearts together. Can you imagine how Paul's greeting to the Philippians would warm your heart and pave the way for marvelous moments of sharing love? Imagine hearing your spouse say to you, "I thank my God upon every remembrance of you" (Philippians 1:3), or, "I thank my

God, making mention of thee always in my prayers" (Philemon 1:4).

The greeting of the brethren at the School of the Prophets is similarly instructive and inspiring: "I salute you in the name of the Lord Jesus Christ, in token or remembrance of the everlasting covenant, to fellowship, in a determination that is fixed, immovable, and unchangeable, to be your friend and brother through the grace of God in the bonds of love, to walk in all the commandments of God blameless, in thanksgiving, forever and ever." (D&C 88:133.)

While such patterns of language may seem stilted or overdone, the pattern of commendation and expressing appreciation and love remains the same. Just image the power of such loving words.

CONCLUSION

What is appropriate preparation for marital intimacy? The Spirit has directed many couples as they have sought the answer to that question for themselves.

What an adventure lies ahead for you and your spouse as you seek to discover activities that bring your spirits to life and invite the Spirit! As you prepare in this way, your ability to experience true marital intimacy will increase.

Chapter 13

"ALTARING" YOUR
MARITAL INTIMACY

Ye are little children, and ye have not as yet understood how great blessings the Father hath in his own hands and prepared for you; and ye cannot bear all things now; nevertheless, be of good cheer, for I will lead you along. The kingdom is yours and the blessings thereof are yours, and the riches of eternity are yours." (D&C 78:17–18.)

Will the Lord lead spouses along as they seek to understand "how great blessings" the Father has prepared for them? Absolutely. If we will ask, we will receive all the help from the Lord we need. We need to ask with the persistence and faith of Moses who said: "I will not cease to call upon God, I have other things to inquire of him." (Moses 1:18.)

We can hear the voice of the Lord in many places: in the mouths of His servants the prophets (see D&C 1:38), in the scriptures, in the temple, and in our homes as we pray and fast. The Lord also speaks to seeking souls in their daily activities—at work, at play, and in conversations with others. Let's consider just two of these possible places where the Lord will lead spouses along as they search for truths and blessings of marital intimacy: the scriptures and the temple.

THE SCRIPTURES

Nephi speaks of likening the scriptures unto ourselves for our profit and learning. In them, we find principles to guide all aspects of our lives. If you are seeking help to draw closer to your spouse, as you read your scriptures with your marriage foremost in your mind, you may be surprised at what insights occur to you.

Just to offer one example of this, let's look closely at chapter 13 of the book of Hebrews, which is full of counsel pertinent to married couples:

1. *"Let brotherly love continue."* (Hebrews 13:1.) In the midst of problems, couples need to "let brotherly love continue." They need to continue to show love and kindness to each other. When spouses remember that because of their divine heritage they are spirit brothers and sisters, walls don't build up quite as high between them during difficult times. They are less likely to punish each other for their difficulties, and more willing to work together on their problems. "Be kind" is the two-word solution to all marital problems offered by Lucille Johnson, a well-known, eighty-year-old marriage and family therapist. (BYU Education Week, August 2000.)

2. *"Be not forgetful to entertain strangers: for thereby some have entertained angels unawares."* (Hebrews 13:2.) When husbands and wives feel like strangers to each other, that should be the first clue for them to start "entertaining" each other. When spouses begin to think about how they would host a stranger in their home, kindness and courtesy, interest and graciousness flow much more readily.

Ask yourself from time to time, in whatever difficult, easy, or neutral situation you're in, "If my spouse were a stranger, how would I handle this situation right now?" Then offer the same words or actions to your spouse as you would if entertaining a stranger. You may even begin to notice "angelic" aspects of your spouse that you have been overlooking.

3. *"Remember them that are in bonds, as bound with them; and them which suffer adversity, as being yourselves also in the body."* (Hebrews 13:3.) When one spouse is held captive by problems, both are held captive. Unfortunately, dual hostages often become dueling hostages!

When one husband was "in bonds" with his anger, his wife was "in bonds" also. Their joint suffering severely decreased their marital intimacy. Things started to change, however, when they started seeing that being "in bonds" together, suffering the adversity of the anger together, could have some positive results. For example, they realized that neither spouse had to feel alone. When the husband started to understand this concept—and remember it—it shored up his strength during weakening times, helping him find courage instead of submitting to his temper. He said, "When I remember that when I yell, berate, and say cruel things—when I let anger rule me instead of me ruling my anger—I am actually choosing to cause my wife to suffer, it almost shocks my system and brings me back to my senses in a moment of weakness."

4. *"Marriage is honourable in all, and the bed undefiled: but whoremongers and adulterers God will judge."* (Hebrews 13:4.) What a helpful message this is to young marrieds who are making the transition from the chastity of a single life to the chastity associated with true marital intimacy. The bed you share with your spouse is not defiled but a blessed place as you increasingly invite the Spirit into your intimate moments and draw closer to each other in the process.

5. *"Let your conversation be without covetousness; and be content with such things as ye have."* (Hebrews 13:5.) How different would your relationship be if you stopped telling your spouse how much you wished things were different? Notice what

happens when you focus on those things you would like to have remain the same about your spouse and your marriage. This is a potentially powerful experience that can open your eyes, hearts, and minds to solutions you have previously overlooked. (See Adams, Pieroy, and Jurich, "Effects of Solution Focused Therapy.")

6. *"For he hath said, I will never leave thee, nor forsake thee. So that we may boldly say, The Lord is my helper, and I will not fear what man shall do unto me."* (Hebrews 13:5–6.) Remember that the Lord will be with you and your spouse—if you invite and seek Him. What more could you want? Does that security of knowing that the Lord will always be with you help you reach out to your spouse—tenaciously and consistently?

The Lord has set the example for spouses to follow: to never leave each other, to not forsake each other. One wife, mother, and grandmother reflected on the strength that came to her own marriage when she realized that she was thoroughly and completely committed to her husband. She reflected: "The moment comes in every marriage—maybe it's in the first year, the tenth year, or the thirtieth year—when the covenant is in force and you say truly to your spouse, 'I will never leave you or forsake you.'"

7. *"But to do good and to communicate forget not."* (Hebrews 13:16.) What an eternal truth! In good times—or in the midst of difficulties and hurt feelings—don't forget "to do good and to communicate"! Keep doing good. And from time to time "do good" by believing that your spouse wants to do good and be good.

Keep talking. Keep sharing what is really in your heart and on your mind. Remember to communicate and, more importantly, to commune. From time to time think about what your spouse may really be trying to say. When you use your most benevolent eyes and ears, what are you able to see and hear? Truly look into your spouse's eyes. What do you see? Truly listen with your heart. What do you hear?

Further Intimacy Instruction Awaits

Other truths about intimacy abound in the scriptures. One woman was grateful that during a very difficult time in her marriage, she received daily specific guidance about how to speak to, feel about, and behave toward her husband. As she prayerfully opened the scriptures, the Spirit opened her eyes, heart, and mind to the words of the Lord, and she was instructed how to open her husband's eyes, heart, and mind to her words. "I was given daily manna from the scriptures for our marriage," she said, "and we were blessed."

When couples approach the scriptures with a prayer in their hearts, "Teach me to love, and teach me about intimacy," there is enough and to spare of truths and tutoring in the written words of the Lord. Spouses can find great treasures of hidden knowledge about intimacy as they follow Alma's advice to his son: "Counsel with the Lord in all thy doings, and he will direct thee for good; yea, when thou liest down at night lie down unto the Lord, that he may watch over you in your sleep; and when thou risest in the morning let thy heart be full of thanks unto God." (Alma 37:37.)

The Temple

When you are feeling weary, worried, lonely, misunderstood, indecisive, discouraged, overwhelmed, overwrought, or underappreciated, you and your spouse need deep immersion in what could be called "celestial therapy."

Celestial therapy involves regularly participating in temple worship and temple service. It involves keeping sacred temple covenants with increasing precision and depth. Celestial therapy is therapy that will make a difference—not only to how spouses live in this world but also to how and where they live in the next.

"There is only one aristocracy that God recognizes," said President George Albert Smith, "and that is the aristocracy of righteousness." (*Sharing the Gospel with Others,* 216.) No one is turned away from the temple who is willing to comply with the Lord's rules for admission. The Lord welcomes all who are willing to show by their actions that they are ready. He Himself has set the requirements. His injunction is simple: "Keep my commandments."

We are the ones who, by our telestial choices, keep ourselves out. And what a tragedy that is! These are days that require us to wake up to the realities of an ever-darkening world. Elder Henry B. Eyring recently warned, "As the forces around us increase in intensity, whatever spiritual strength was once sufficient will not be enough." (*Ensign,* October 1999, 9.) Whatever spiritual strength was once sufficient to forge a great marital relationship may not be enough. However, all the strength and healing that will help us overcome the problems and pains of this world, and the constraints to marital intimacy, is found within the doors of the temple.

The Savior waits with open arms and eternal healing to help us overcome those problems that are to be overcome, and to endure those that are to be endured. He is waiting to help. What are we waiting for? The Lord is the Master Healer. He has boundless power to heal our minds and marriages, our hearts and homes. And what an assurance it is to seek help from Him who knows us better than we know ourselves.

Because of the Savior's love for us, He wants to offer us all He knows. He offers us His eternal laws and ordinances with their accompanying joy and peace. It seems true that the more laws we know—and, more important, the more laws we live— the more joy and peace we can experience within our marriages. The laws the Lord offers us in His temple bring us out of the world and ever closer to heaven. As we live them, we rise above the telestial living that predictably brings such grief and darkness into our lives.

In D&C 109:22 the Lord tells us of four priesthood blessings that accompany faithfully keeping our temple covenants. He promises that when we go forth from His house we can leave:

1. armed with His power,
2. with His name upon us,
3. with His glory round about us, and
4. with His angels having charge over us.

Through these blessings, we can build marriages that will build Zion.

What difference can these promised temple blessings make in spouses' lives? Let's consider, as an example, how the Lord's power and name can influence a man and his wife who are suffering from years of being under the influence of the husband's rage and criticism. He feels misunderstood and rejected. His wife feels alone and worthless.

What happens as this husband begins to participate regularly in temple worship? According to the Lord's promises, he has the opportunity to be armed with His power. Thus fortified, he has the power to see—perhaps to see himself as never before. The house of the Lord is indeed a house of revelation. When this man reads Jacob 2:35, this time it's personal: "Ye have broken the [heart] of your tender [wife], and lost the confidence of your children, because of your bad examples before them."

This husband could also plead for and be given power to cast away contention that prohibits the Spirit of the Lord from being present. In this way he can understand why, even though he feels love for his wife, she has not experienced his love. The Spirit is the messenger of love. When the Spirit flees because of contention, so does the perception of love. However, now armed with the power of the Lord, this man can grow in his ability to do what he has previously not been able to do: apologize, commend, forgive, and express love.

How can the second promise of the Lord—that His name will be upon us as we leave His house—help this man? What happens when he leaves the temple and remembers that his every action is now done in the name of the Lord? What happens when he is tempted to yell or criticize?

As this man applies his sacred covenants day by day, we can predict that his confidence will wax stronger and stronger in the presence of the Lord and his wife. His heart will not be set upon himself or the things of the world, but rather will be turned to his wife. His concern will be to do everything he can do to enliven his wife's spirit and to strengthen her heart.

One or two trips to the temple won't bring these results, but as this man continues to immerse himself in temple worship, he will experience a power and protection unlike anything he has ever experienced before. Because of Christ's protective power, he will courageously withstand the impulses of retaliation and win his fight against fighting. He will be able to contend against contention. And his wife will rise up and call him blessed. (See Proverbs 31:28.)

And what is true for this man and his anger is true for other problems that plague marriages and can work against increased intimacy:

- a wife and her procrastination
- a husband and his lying
- a wife and her unforgiveness
- a husband and his struggle with pornography
- a wife and her battle with the bulge
- a husband and his career crisis
- a wife and her grief

For every problem in our lives, there is power and knowledge in the temple to help us.

THE LORD'S ALTAR

Celestial therapy heals with the help of the Lord's altar. What seems impossible to solve in your own life or marriage right now? Put your biggest problem on the Lord's altar. Lay it down. The Lord can alter whatever we are willing to put on His altar.

One woman struggled with chronic bitterness toward her husband. Longing for change, she fasted and prayed. With the power and knowledge she gained through temple worship, she learned how to lay her bitterness on the Lord's altar. Her husband noticed an almost immediate difference in her behavior toward him. With the bitterness removed, she was able to reach out to him in ways she had not done for many years. He responded in kind, and the intimacy in their marriage dramatically increased.

A husband wrote about taking all things pertaining to their marriage to the altar of the Lord. He wrote, "We can count on both hands the number of times in twelve years of marriage that we have retired for the evening without kneeling together, hand-in-hand by our bedside, and thanked and petitioned Heavenly Father on behalf of our marriage and family and each other. When there has been strife between us, the prayer for our marriage relationship has been 'Please forgive us for our pettiness and selfishness, and help us to let go of our hurts and be joined once again in unity of purpose.'

"We don't think that it is necessary to always be in formal prayer together as a couple in order to be at the altar before the Lord. Just as we can have a prayer continually in our hearts, a covenant marriage allows us, as a couple, to be continually before Him at the altar, if our actions and thoughts are in keeping with our temple covenants.

"One night we watched a movie together that brought up a lot of emotions for me. I was able to share with my wife at that time that I adore her and that I'm willing to do whatever it takes to be with her eternally. I also told her that, just like the man in the movie who had to make many changes on behalf of his marriage, it has all been worth it for me. My wife said that she understood how many changes I've made in order to come into this marriage relationship as fully as I have, and that she honored those changes and my choice to do so. I believe that during these moments of most intimate sharing, we are at the altar in the Lord's eyes. I especially feel that way because afterward, I often have the feeling of homesickness for my heavenly home.

"I guess for me the most important thing about coming before the Lord as a couple is this: While it is certainly appropriate and necessary for each individual in a marriage to continue in personal development and progression, if the marriage is to be sealed up and continue beyond this sphere, each party must realize that they are part of a separate entity created by holy sealing powers.

"Many problems in today's marriages lie in the futile and frustrating efforts of men and women trying to remain as individuals in a marriage where God has commanded that they be one with another. Just as we must surrender ourselves to Christ and take upon ourselves His name, as husbands and wives we must surrender our 'aloneness' for the 'oneness' that an eternal marriage has to offer. If we don't, we can be married and have happiness to a degree in this life, but the marriage unit can't continue and be an eternal one."

This husband and wife had altered their lives through their continuous efforts to place their marriage on the altar of the Lord.

CELESTIAL THERAPY HEALS SPOUSES

Celestial therapy can heal spouses and increase their ability to give and receive love through its freeing, revealing, and comforting influence.

1. Celestial therapy heals us as it frees us.

Through the freeing influence of celestial therapy, we can save time and energy—and perhaps even money! Think of how that could help your marriage! How can celestial therapy do this? Because after celestial therapy, many ideas, projects, and passions that previously consumed our time, energy, and financial resources are no longer on our "wanna do" or "gotta do" lists.

When a temple was built in Edmonton, Alberta, Canada, there was a grand response from the Saints as they rededicated their lives to serving the Lord and their families. One sister said, "We've all sold our recreational vehicles, and now we're all happily working in the temple!"

Celestial therapy can also free us and save us time and energy by turning many "hot issues" of the world into non-issues for us. These days, one wonders exactly how many talk shows, prime-time news panels, books, and government programs it takes to resolve a "hot issue." Try celestial therapy instead: Take one "hot world topic." Consider it in the light of the eternal teachings of the temple. What is the result? Most often, it becomes a non-issue. This is also often the case with marital "issues."

Celestial therapy can free us and our ancestors. As we participate in the privilege of proxy ordinances to free our kindred dead, we are freed ourselves. We are freer when we leave the temple than when we entered: freer to do what the Lord requires of us, freer to discern good from evil, freer to fill the measure of our creation and experience joy, freer to solve our problems, and freer to give our will to the Lord. We are freer to be better men and women. President Hinckley has said: "I make a promise to you that every time you come to the temple you will be a better man or woman when you leave than you were when you came. That is a promise. I believe it with all my heart." (*Church News*, January 29, 2000, 5.)

We are also freer to put aside telestial behaviors that shrink our spirits and grieve the Spirit. Eliza R. Snow and Zina Diantha Huntington Young were great advocates of temple worship. Was it the effects of Zina's temple experiences that allowed her to respond lovingly when she was told that a certain woman didn't like her: "Well, I love her—and she can't help herself." (Peterson and Gaunt, *Elect Ladies*, 57.)

When your spouse is unkind, judges you unfairly, or persistently undermines your best efforts, can you respond like Zina? Through celestial therapy you can.

2. Celestial therapy can heal us through what it reveals to us.

Celestial therapy can give us insights into ourselves and our spouses that we never considered before, and it can tell us what to do in difficult situations. The Lord generously manifests to us those things we are seeking—just as soon as He perceives we are ready. At times His revelations show us even more than we believe we requested.

A husband prayed fervently during his temple worship for further purifying so he could fill the measure of his creation, but he wasn't prepared for the Lord's refining instructions. During the endowment session and for a full week following, the whisperings of the Spirit invited him to uncover the pride in his life. He was embarrassed to find obvious pride manifested in his judgmental and unforgiving attitude toward his wife. But things really started to change when he was able to see pride as the root of so many things he struggled with not only in his marriage but in other aspects of his life as well. He realized that pride invited him to believe that the Lord's laws of health really didn't apply to him, that he didn't have to exercise and eat properly to have increased health and fitness. Pride made him believe he was above that—and thus pride invited excessive pounds and bad health to become part of his life.

This man also learned that on occasions when he felt left out of his wife's extended family gatherings, it was really his pride telling him that they should be more interested in him. Pride's myopic stance isolated him. He was amazed to recognize the relationship between feelings of low self-worth, selfishness, and pride.

A wife was continually in emotional upheaval and even despair because of a difficult relationship with her mother-in-law. The conflict was negatively affecting her relationship with her husband. By immersing herself in intensive celestial therapy, she was able to give up defending herself and making critical comments about her supposed enemy. How? One day, as this woman was reflecting on her temple covenants and this agonizing situation, a question came to her mind that totally changed her view of her mother-in-law's difficult behavior. The question was, "How would I respond to my mother-in-law's gross misinterpretations of everything I do if I were to discover that one of her premortal assignments was to help me prove myself to the Lord—and, in the process, truly come to know myself?"

She mused further and wondered, "What if my mother-in-law's premortal commitment to me and love for me is actually the driving force behind her troubling behavior? What if pre-mortally she was so devoted to me that she was willing to behave in such a way as to even risk not receiving love from me here on earth? If this were true, how could I restrain myself from running to her and thanking her? How could I withhold my love from her anymore?"

These celestial thoughts freed this woman's mind and heart and allowed her to extend kindness and love—even in the midst of continuing false accusations from her mother-in-law. And she and her husband moved forward in finding more joy and love and peace in their marriage.

3. Celestial therapy can heal spouses by comforting them.

One way spouses are comforted is through anticipating future joys. Celestial therapy was the healing balm for a woman ravaged with the pain of childlessness, the grief of believing that both she and her body had betrayed her loving husband, and the anguish induced by the all-seeing eyes of her neighbors—who cruelly questioned her devotion to home, family, and the Church.

One day in temple worship she was given a comforting thought that her children were indeed waiting on the other side of the veil for her. She had been told something similar before by friends but had never really believed it—passing it off as a trite way to dismiss and even negate her pain. But because of previous temple experiences, she knew this thought was a personal truth mercifully given to her by Him who really knew.

Her grief and pain fell away, and she started to think of all the ways she could groom herself as a wonderful mother in this life by nurturing and bearing with others, even in their most unlovable moments. With majestic confidence borne of celestial tutoring, she continues to move through her life, blessing others' lives and no longer shrinking from the violets offered in church on Mother's Day.

Celestial therapy can indeed heal spouses through its freeing, revealing, and comforting power. Inside the temple, the Lord's altar is part of celestial therapy. When we depart from the temple, celestial therapy continues as we leave with the Lord's power and name upon us—and with His glory and angels round about us.

Through celestial therapy we can increasingly come to know the Savior and to love Him above everyone and everything else. Such singleness of heart was spoken by a young husband and father as he named and blessed his newborn son: "Pedro, you will know your wife because she will love the Lord more than she loves you."

Truly, the ultimate motivation in our lives comes when we want to draw closer to the Lord than we ever have—closer to Him than to anyone else. And thus He brings us closer to everyone. As spouses center their love and lives on the Savior and His temple, they will experience an anchoring and a direction in their marital intimacy that is unsurpassed.

STARTING ANEW BY "ALTARING" YOUR MARRIAGE

Some couples face the daunting task of starting anew with their marriages following very difficult times in their relationships. Some couples are so discouraged and overwhelmed by their problems that they just want to give up. One bishop said, "I tell young couples who say they want a divorce, 'I'm sure the Lord wants you to divorce as well.' This catches their attention, and then I continue: 'I'm sure He wants you to divorce yourself from the thoughts and behaviors that have prevented you from really developing a marriage yet.' I tell them that I agree with them that they need a new relationship—a new relationship with each other."

One couple had struggled with a myriad of problems during their twenty-five years of marriage. Their journey through, not around, their problems required everything they could each give—spiritually, physically, emotionally, mentally. They worked—

sweat and tears kind of work—as a couple and individually to do many of the things that have been written about in this book.

After MUCH praying, fasting, reading, writing, reflecting, regretting, talking, listening, giving, receiving, defending, commending, repenting, forgiving, apologizing, acknowledging, succeeding, failing, trying again, uniting, fighting, seeking, silencing, dreaming, despairing, planning, worrying, holding back, holding on . . . the husband wrote a letter of commitment and invitation to his wife—words she had been longing to hear for most of their marriage. It began:

"What I am proposing is that you take my hand and together we start a new life by leaving the past behind and moving forward together with Jesus Christ as our anchor and centerpiece and the first in our lives, and then with each other as the most important element of our joint thoughts and actions."

He went on to describe his commitment to change and his desire to unite his life with hers in every aspect, and closed with an invitation:

"I pray and beg of you to join me in this new adventure for the rest of our earthly lives and into eternity. I am in love with you and I will always love you with all my heart. In spite of our past problems, there is no one else on this earth who stirs my soul with passion, love, compassion, and charity as do you.

"With all my love."

ALL THAT HE CAN DO

The words of Elder Howard W. Hunter are true: "If Jesus lays his hands upon a marriage, it lives." (In Conference Report, October 1979, 93.) As you seek the Savior's help to strengthen your marriage and increase your marital intimacy:

• He will give you and your spouse new hearts. Listen to His words: "A new heart also will I give you, and a new spirit will I put within you: and I will take away the stony heart out of your flesh, and I will give you an heart of flesh." (Ezekiel 36:26–27.)

• He will purify your passions through the gift of the Holy Ghost. He will pour His Spirit into your soul (see Jacob 7:8) so that your passions will be pure. Passion that is pure isn't manipulative or feigned; it is not contaminated with anger, resentments, unforgiveness, or dishonesty; it is not ruled by the deceptions of the ruler of darkness. Pure passion grows out of a desire to unite more completely with your spouse and to draw closer to the Lord. Pure passion can heal and lift, nourish and nurture.

The Savior is a God with body, parts, and passions. Purified passions will continue to be magnified throughout eternity. Purity and passion truly do belong together forever. Orson Pratt taught: "When the sons and daughters of the Most High God come forth in the morning of the first resurrection, this principle of love will exist in their bosoms just as it exists here, only intensified according to the increased knowledge and understanding they possess; hence, they will be capacitated to enjoy the relationship of husband and wife . . . in a hundred fold degree greater than they could in mortality." (In *Journal of Discourses*, 13:187.)

• He will help you fill your mission to raise up a righteous spouse unto Him. Your mission will require your whole heart and may require you to learn a language you have never learned before: the language of love. Or you may need to teach your spouse this foreign language because he or she has never learned it. As you pray for the Savior's assistance, you'll have success because He will loose your tongue and give you utterance.

Your mission as a spouse involves converting a man (or woman) into a husband (or wife). Only in the presence of a real husband does a woman arise as a real wife. Only in the presence of a real wife does a man arise as a real husband. So if you want your husband to be more of a husband, try being more of a wife. And vice versa.

• As you seek to strengthen your marriage and "counsel with the Lord in all thy doings, . . . he will direct thee for good." (Alma

37:37.) And when appropriate He will send angels to minister to you to give you "skill and understanding." (Daniel 9:22.)

• He will never leave you alone in your searching to strengthen your marriage, but will "be on your right hand and on your left" (D&C 84:91) as you increasingly come out of the world and invite Him into your efforts to overlap your world with that of your spouse, and thus co-create your own "new" world where true marital intimacy abides.

GUIDELINES FOR APPLYING
THESE TRUTHS

Knowledge is power when it is applied. Watch what happens in your marriage as you and your spouse:

1. Seek confirmation from the Spirit about which of the ideas offered in this book are indeed the spiritual truths about intimacy that will strengthen *your* marriage. Then do as Paul counseled: "Continue thou in the things which thou hast learned and hast been assured of, knowing of whom thou hast learned them." (2 Timothy 3:14.)

2. Day by day put into practice your unfolding understanding of the spiritual truths about intimacy. Take just one truth—either one you found in this book or one that you have been drawn to elsewhere. Ask yourself, "If I really were to believe this particular spiritual truth about marital intimacy, what would I do?" Then do it. Watch your spouse's response and notice how you feel. Then try applying another truth. And then another.

3. Relentlessly pray for the Spirit to purify your passions. In your morning and evening prayers, individually and together, pray for the Holy Ghost to increase, enlarge, expand, and purify all your natural passions and affections. (See Parley P. Pratt, *Key to the Science of Theology,* 61.) Then live so that He can.

4. Come out of the world more and more so you can enjoy marital intimacy that is truly not of this world. From time to time review the appendix: "A Synopsis of God-Ordained Marital

Intimacy versus Worldly Sex." Talk with your spouse about what the two of you are doing, or need to do, to increase your experiences with God-ordained marital intimacy.

I believe that as you and your spouse follow these four application guidelines, your marriage will be strengthened and your marital intimacy will be filled with more love, light, power, peace, and joy than you have ever imagined.

And the Savior Jesus Christ Himself will anoint your marriage with the "oil of gladness." (Hebrews 1:9.)

Spirit communes with spirit,
thought meets with thought,
soul blends with soul,
in all the raptures of
mutual, pure and eternal love.

—Parley P. Pratt,
Key to the Science of Theology, 75

A Synopsis of God-Ordained Marital Intimacy versus Worldly Sex

God-Ordained Marital Intimacy

Helps put off the natural man

Under the influence of the Spirit

Involves Spirit-enhanced passions

Loving

Soulful union is the goal

Eternal

Involves a husband and a wife

Worldly Sex

Accommodates the "natural man"

Under the influence of the world and the adversary

Involves carnal, sensual, devilish passions

Lustful

Sexual union is the goal

Erotic

Involves all permutations and combinations of men, women, even children

GOD-ORDAINED MARITAL INTIMACY	WORLDLY SEX
Sanctioned following legal and lawful marriage	Okay anytime
Blessed by the Lord	Very politically correct
Sanctifying	Sinful
Fun and exciting, joyful, delightful, comforting, loving, calming, and sustaining	Fun and exciting momentarily, demoralizing and depressing later
Generates love	Kills love
Enlightens and enlivens spirits	Darkens spirits
Prayer, fasting, scripture reading, gratitude often involved	Alcohol and drugs often involved
Strengthens relationships	Ruins relationships
Honors men and women	Degrades men and women
The body is the great prize of mortal life	The body is a plaything
The greater the union of lives, the greater the intimate experience	No union of lives, only bodies
Embedded in truths	Filled with lies
Involves anything that brings spouses' spirits to life and invites the Spirit	Involves any and all forms of sexual gratification
A grand and glorious experience that will continue eternally for covenant-keeping couples	A total obsession; men and women wish they could have sex forever

GOD-ORDAINED MARITAL INTIMACY	WORLDLY SEX
Unites the bodies *and* the spirits of a husband and wife	Involves any two bodies
Exquisite care taken that activities don't offend the Spirit	If it "turns you on," go for it!
Brings forth loving desires that fulfill	Stirs up lustful desires that are never satisfied
Spouses feel more like a couple, more loved, more appreciated, and more cared for following	Individuals feel used, abused, more lonely after
Supports, heals, and hallows lives	Ravages and eventually ruins lives
Personal revelation encouraged	Experimentation encouraged
Is partaken of	Is participated in
Private and sacred	Seen and discussed everywhere
Brings you wisdom, light, and love	Dulls your senses and sensibilities
A process	A product
Unites spouses and is built on unity	Separates individuals
Invites other loving, caring and supportive behaviors outside bedroom	Not related to what happens outside bedroom
Sacred language used	Foul language used

GOD-ORDAINED MARITAL INTIMACY	WORLDLY SEX
Rejoiced in	Joked about
Keeps commandments and covenants	Breaks commandments and covenants
Increases the ability to keep and honor all commandments and covenants	Increases the likelihood of breaking other commandments and covenants
Is commanded and commended by the Lord	Is rejected by the Lord
Involves pure, natural passions	Involves impure, unnatural passions
Is the foundation of endless worlds	Supports an entire commercial industry

Sources Cited

Adams, J. F., F. P. Pieroy, and J. A. Jurich. "Effects of Solution Focused Therapy's 'Formula First Session Task' on Compliance and Outcome in Family Therapy." *Journal of Marriage and Family Therapy*, vol. 17, no. 3 (1990), 277–90.

Benson, Ezra Taft. "The Law of Chastity." *BYU 1987–88 Devotional and Fireside Speeches*. Provo, Utah: Brigham Young University, 1988.

Brown, Victor L., Jr. *Human Intimacy*. Salt Lake City: Bookcraft, 1981.

Callister, Tad R. *The Infinite Atonement*. Salt Lake City: Deseret Book, 2000.

Gottman, John. *What Predicts Divorce? The Relationship Between Marital Processes and Marital Outcomes*. Hillsdale, N.J.: Erlbaum, 1994.

———, and Nan Silver. *Why Marriages Succeed or Fail*. New York: Simon and Schuster, 1994.

Harper, James M., and Wendy L. Watson. Unpublished questionnaire. Brigham Young University, 1996.

Hinckley, Bryant S. *Sermons and Missionary Services of Melvin J. Ballard*. Salt Lake City: Deseret Book, 1949.

Hinckley, Gordon B. *Teachings of Gordon B. Hinckley*. Salt Lake City: Deseret Book, 1997.

———. *Standing for Something*. New York: Times Books, 2000.

Holland, Jeffrey R. "Of Souls, Symbols, and Sacraments." In *Morality*, compilation. Salt Lake City: Bookcraft, 1992, 152–66.

Hunter, Howard W. *That We Might Have Joy*. Salt Lake City: Deseret Book, 1994.

Hymns of The Church of Jesus Christ of Latter-day Saints. Salt Lake City: The Church of Jesus Christ of Latter-day Saints, 1985.

Kimball, Heber C. *1844 Journal*. Archives Division, Historical

Department, The Church of Jesus Christ of Latter-day Saints, Salt Lake City, Utah.

Kimball, Spencer W. *BYU Speeches of the Year, 1976.* Provo, Utah: Brigham Young University, 1977.

———. *The Teachings of Spencer W. Kimball.* Edited by Edward L. Kimball. Salt Lake City: Bookcraft, 1982.

Larson, Jeffry H. *Should We Stay Together?* San Francisco: Jossey-Bass, 2000.

Lewis, C. S. *The Screwtape Letters.* London: Collins Fontana Books, 1942.

Madsen, Truman G. *Four Essays on Love.* Salt Lake City: Bookcraft, 1971.

———. *The Presidents of the Church.* Audiotape series, 15 cassettes. Salt Lake City: Bookcraft, 1999.

Maturana, H. R. "Biology, Emotions and Culture." Videotape presentation. Calgary, Canada: Vanry & Associates, November 1992.

———. "The Calgary-Chile Coupling." Transcript of telephone conversation, Calgary, Canada, 1988.

———, and Francisco G. Varela. *The Tree of Knowledge: The Biological Roots of Human Understanding,* rev. ed. Boston: Shambhala, 1992.

Maxwell, Neal A. *Notwithstanding My Weakness.* Salt Lake City: Deseret Book, 1981.

McConkie, Bruce R. *The Mortal Messiah,* 4 vols. Salt Lake City: Deseret Book, 1979–1981.

McConkie, Joseph Fielding. *Gospel Symbolism.* Salt Lake City: Bookcraft, 1985.

Medalie, J., and V. Goldbourt. "Angina Predictors among 10,000 Men." *American Journal of Medicine,* vol. 60 (1976): 910–21.

Millet, Robert L. *Alive in Christ: The Miracle of Spiritual Rebirth.* Salt Lake City: Deseret Book, 1997.

Packer, Boyd K. *The Things of the Soul.* Salt Lake City: Bookcraft, 1996.

Paulus, Trina. *Hope for the Flowers.* New York: Paulist Press, 1972.

Peterson, Janet, and LaRene Gaunt. *Elect Ladies.* Salt Lake City: Deseret Book, 1990.

Pratt, Parley P. *Autobiography of Parley P. Pratt.* Salt Lake City: Deseret Book, 1985, 280.

———. *Key to the Science of Theology.* Salt Lake City: Deseret Book, 1965.

Scriptures of the Church: Selections from the Encyclopedia of Mormonism. Edited by Daniel H. Ludlow. Salt Lake City: Deseret Book, 1995.

Smith, George Albert. *Sharing the Gospel with Others.* Salt Lake City: Deseret Book, 1948.

Smith, Joseph, Jr. *Teachings of the Prophet Joseph Smith.* Selected and arranged by Joseph Fielding Smith. Salt Lake City: Deseret Book, 1976.

———. *Discourses of the Prophet Joseph Smith.* Compiled by Alma P. Burton. Salt Lake City: Deseret Book, 1986.

Smith, Joseph F. *Gospel Doctrine.* Salt Lake City: Deseret Book, 1939.

Snow, Lorenzo. *Official Journal of Lorenzo Snow.* Archives Division, Historical Department, The Church of Jesus Christ of Latter-day Saints, Salt Lake City, Utah.

Timmerman, G. M. "A Concept Analysis of Intimacy." *Issues in Mental Health Nursing,* vol. 12 (1991): 19–30.

Tomm, Karl. "Towards a Cybernetic-Systems Approach to Family Therapy." In D. S. Freeman, ed., *Perspectives on Family Therapy.* Vancouver, British Columbia. Butterworths, 1980.

Watzlawick, Paul, Janet Beavin Bavelas, and Don D. Jackson. *Pragmatics of Human Communication.* New York: W. W. Norton, 1967.

Widtsoe, John A. *Evidences and Reconciliations: Aids to Faith in a Modern Day.* Salt Lake City: Bookcraft, 1943.

Wright, L. M., W. L. Watson, and J. M. Bell. *Beliefs: The Heart of Healing in Families and Illness.* New York: Basic Books, 1996.

Young, Brigham. *Discourses of Brigham Young.* Selected by John A. Widtsoe. Salt Lake City: Deseret Book, 1941.

Zunin, Leonard, and Natalie Zunin. *Contact: The First Four Minutes.* New York: Ballantine Books, 1972.

INDEX